Cebio

T5-AQQ-805

You Are Worth It

NOV -- 2019

You Are Worth It

Building a Life Worth Fighting For

Kyle Carpenter
and Don Yaeger

HARPER LUXE

An Imprint of HarperCollinsPublishers

YOU ARE WORTH IT. Copyright © 2019 by Kyle Carpenter and Don Yaeger. All rights reserved. Printed in the United States of America. No part of this book may be used or reproduced in any manner whatsoever without written permission except in the case of brief quotations embodied in critical articles and reviews. For information, address HarperCollins Publishers, 195 Broadway, New York, NY 10007.

HarperCollins books may be purchased for educational, business, or sales promotional use. For information, please e-mail the Special Markets Department at SPsales@harpercollins.com.

FIRST HARPERLUXE EDITION

ISBN: 978-0-06-294424-5

HarperLuxe™ is a trademark of HarperCollins Publishers.

Library of Congress Cataloging-in-Publication Data is available upon request.

19 20 21 22 23 LSC 10 9 8 7 6 5 4 3 2 1

To my parents, Jim and Robin, and my brothers, Price and Peyton.

Thank you will never be enough for the journey you have traveled and endured with me, but just know that your love helped comfort me, heal me, and give me life (again). I am thankful for you every day. I love you.

—KC

To Jeanette, Will, and Maddie: You make every day WORTH it! I love you all.

—DY

Contents

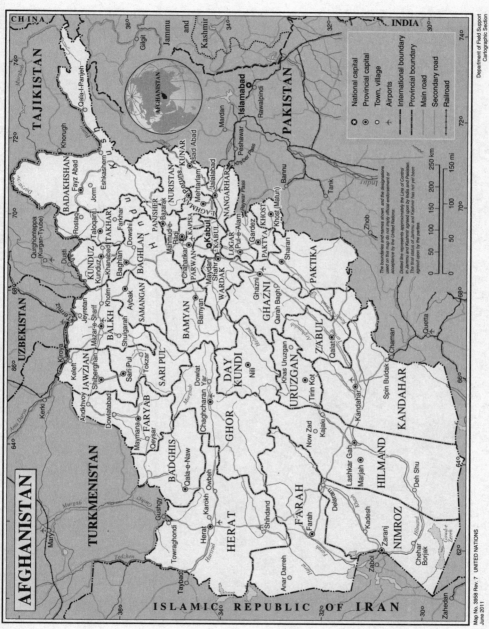

AFGHANISTAN

Map No. 3958 Rev. 7 UNITED NATIONS
June 2011

Department of Field Support
Cartographic Section

You Are Worth It

Introduction
You Are Worth It

I hopped in the black sedan and closed the door. Yet another ride to the airport. This time I was headed to London.

The moment I hit the seat I began scanning through various emails of tickets, reservations, and confirmations to make sure every step of my trip over the next seven days would be as smooth as possible. But with each tap of the screen came a comment from the driver; he clearly wanted to talk. I put my phone down to chat with Bobby. He had come to America at a young age, with his parents, from Pakistan. He proceeded to tell me that he became an Uber driver after getting burned out as a banker who specialized in mortgages, because it was stressful for him to deal with people's homes and their livelihoods on a daily basis. As his story unfolded, we connected. I could relate to feeling burned out, if for different reasons. I appreciated his openness and honesty, and as the conversation continued I decided to share my journey and struggle with him. He listened intently and when I was finished, he said the same five words I have heard countless times.

"Thank you for your service."

The phrase has prompted some discussion within the veteran community because it is so predictable, almost reflexive. It's become filler language for when people don't know what else to say to you, but they want to say *something*. I know some vets are bothered by it because it can feel hollow, as if the person is just saying it out of obligation or habit, or the vets feel that they are being valued solely for their military service and not for anything else.

Personally, I don't mind the phrase. That person didn't have to take time out of their day to say anything to me, but they did, and that means something. I usually just say, "Thank you very much. I really appreciate that."

But that day, on the way to the airport, I responded as I never had before. As Bobby said, "Thank you for your service," I replied, "You're worth it."

He paused as he looked at me intently in the rear-view mirror. To be honest, I paused, too. *Why did I just say that?* I had heard the phrase before, but never said it to anyone. How would it come across to someone else? I didn't know how Bobby would take it, but in that moment, I wanted him to know that his family, his freedom, his rights, just the simple fact that he was a human being, meant that he was worth sacrificing for . . . and that's what I have come to realize serving in the military means to me.

The last few minutes of our ride were silent but as we approached the airport, he said to me, "My parents are retired and they have had a peaceful and happy life. I received a great education and I will never experience the struggles my parents faced. That is because of you and our military, for which I will always be thankful. I will pray that God will bless your journey, my brother."

As Bobby from Pakistan pulled away, I took a moment to reflect on the encounter, the twist of fate, that had suddenly pulled all the fragmented pieces into focus for me. I'd said, "You're worth it." And I'd meant it.

As time has passed, and the more I've said it, the more I realize how deeply true the words are: *You are worth it. You are.* You are worth protecting, you are worth fighting for, you are worth time in a hospital bed and deep scars on my body because all Americans—and the people of Afghanistan, and so many people around the world who go to bed at night wishing to one day taste freedom and peace—have inherent worth as human beings. If we don't spend our time on this earth looking out for one another, what are we really doing with our lives?

I want to be straight with you: My goal isn't just to make people think about the "long run," but to look even beyond that. How are what they are doing today and the impact they are making on their world right now going to persist? Some of the greatest deeds, work, recognition, and impact do not come to fruition until long after their human creators are gone. It's the whole idea of "planting trees whose shade you will never enjoy." Or, as one character says in *Cloud Atlas*, "Our lives are not our own. We are bound to others, past and present, and by each crime and every kindness, we birth our future."

On a more personal level, you are worth whatever you want to invest in yourself. You are worth pushing through whatever is holding you back, whatever challenges you are facing, whatever seemingly insurmountable odds are staring back at you. You are worth pursuing the happiness you search for when you look in the mirror.

I am worth it, too, and that is why I fought to rebuild my life into something even greater than it was before a grenade changed everything for me.

It might seem natural to divide my life into two parts, before the explosion and after, but that would give the bad guy who wanted to kill me too much power over my story. I am about so much more than that one moment. The explosion is simply one event in a lifetime of events, all of which have shaped me, changed me, made me grow, and made me who I am. And the life I am living now—even as I am continuing to build it—is one I love.

I am worth it. And so are you.

Chapter 1
Afghanistan

Marjah, Afghanistan. Marines only half-jokingly compare it to the surface of the moon. There are signs of life—the landscape and villages are interwoven with lush agricultural fields, tree lines, and irrigation canals—but other parts are bleak, rocky, and dusty. One of the first things you notice about the place is the dust. It consumes you. From the ground to the air, from your gear to your throat, the dust takes over. With every step, a little cloud of dust puffs up under your boot, no matter how hard-packed the ground is. By 2010, after nine years of a U.S. presence in Afghanistan, the ground at the major bases was about as hard-packed as could be.

The temperature is somehow more dramatic than you expect. It's hotter in summer than you imagined was possible, and it's colder in winter than you are prepared for. The temperature extremes are more evident at night. In September you have to drink a bottle or two of water before bed to make up for what you're going to sweat out in your sleep, but by the start of November, your cold-weather gear can't keep the frigidness from creeping into your feet during night watches, to the point that movement becomes slow and difficult. For a U.S. Marine in Afghanistan, you might as well be on the moon.

By November 2010, the 2nd Battalion 9th Marines, or "2/9," had been in the country for four months. I had enlisted not quite two years earlier, at the very end of 2008, just as U.S. and allied joint operations were ramping up. Many of the Marines in 2/9 had joined around that time, too, and for most of us, this was our first combat deployment. We were physically trained, mentally hardened, and in a naive way, excited. We had all gone into the military with our eyes open. We knew we would almost certainly be inserted into an active war zone—but it's impossible to ever be fully prepared for it. As a small-town Southern kid just a month past my twenty-first birthday, the situation in Afghanistan represented everything I believed in and nothing I had expected. I had grown up saying the Pledge of Allegiance every day in school and believing that "liberty and justice *for all*" was an ideal worth fighting for. To me, it meant rooting out the bad guys who had killed almost three thousand people from ninety countries— people of every race, religion, and ethnicity—on September 11, 2001, as well as, hopefully, ending the brutal Taliban rule that had oppressed and killed so many Afghan people.

We had hydration packs to combat the extreme heat, and cold-weather gear to try to conserve what heat we could at night. We were issued phrase books to help us engage in basic communication with the locals, and try to understand their customs. But as thoroughly as the Marine Corps had prepared us tactically, the culture shock was overwhelming; we'd been transported into a world of mud homes and villages that went back hundreds of years, dominated by ways of life that probably went back thousands.

If I had to summarize Marjah in one word, it would be "harsh." There is a harshness to the land, to the climate, to the way of life . . . and to some of the people. Like the guys who had been throwing grenades at us for the past two days. Then again, that may not be fair; some of the guys who placed IEDs (improvised explosive devices) or shot at us only did it because the Taliban threatened to kill their family if they didn't . . . but I guess that kind of proves my point. Afghanistan is harsh.

The grenades were actually a new thing for us; up to that point, the Taliban had mostly sent bullets in our direction, and the occasional rocket. Grenades are tricky because for them to be effective you have to be in pretty close proximity to your target—no farther away than you can throw. Thankfully most of the bad guys we'd encountered so far had seemed to want to keep their distance. But we were in a new compound now, having taken it on November 19, and the setup was not exactly what we would have chosen.

There were terrible blind spots in our position, which allowed bad guys to get much closer to us than they would have normally attempted. But up until the grenades started, I hardly even noticed the noise of them shooting at us anymore. There were certain sounds I never would have imagined that I could tune out, like AK-47s being shot at me with the intent to kill, but at some point, your brain starts registering certain input as more of a nuisance than a threat. Besides, bullets were not our main concern. We were focused on avoiding the IEDs that were stretched across roadways and walking paths and inside of walls. They had taken quite a toll on 2/9. On September 30, Lance Corporal

Timothy M. Jackson had been killed by an IED. Then in mid-November, IEDs had taken out two more of our guys. By the end of our seven-month deployment, we'd lost almost two dozen men—amazing Marines and sailors, all of them.

One of those remarkable Marines was our squad leader, Zach Stinson, who stepped on an IED that had been placed underground near a wall that separated two villages. The scariest thing about an IED is that, without a metal detector, a well-placed one can be almost impossible to spot, even in broad daylight. You're lucky if the person who placed the IED is inexperienced or lazy because they will leave red flags, like disturbed dirt or a small trash pile that looks like it might have been constructed to hide something.

On November 9, at about 1:00 P.M., we were walking on patrol through one of the dried-up irrigation canals that crisscrossed the landscape. We were scanning the terrain for Taliban and making our way toward the next town we needed to secure—when another dreaded explosion went off.

The shock wave of the blast rippled through our patrol.

I was the fourth man in the patrol. The cloud of dust engulfed me as the debris rained down. The stomach-wrenching curiosity of who had been hit began to sink in. It took a few seconds to locate Stinson because he had been blown about fifteen feet and was on the other side of the wall of the canal. We found him folded in half like a lawn chair. His one remaining foot was up by his head and his legs were mangled.

Christopher "Doc" Frend, our corpsman (the Marine Corps term for a combat medic), quickly evaluated the scene and announced, "I think Stinson is dead." It didn't seem possible anyone could survive that.

Incredibly, Stinson called out, "I'm not dead. I just can't move."

Doc rushed over to him to administer triage care while other Marines called in a medical evacuation helicopter (medevac) and our squad moved to provide cover. Just as we got into position, insurgents opened fire and began their attack; they often attack after an IED blast because they know that our corpsman will be with the casualties, leaving us exposed and vulnerable.

Doc tried to pull Stinson to a safe location while I laid down fire to suppress the shooters. Two other Marines rushed to help Doc drag Stinson to safety behind the other canal wall. As they did, they realized that one of his legs was no longer attached to his body; what was left simply stayed on the ground as he was dragged around the corner.

While Doc applied tourniquets, Stinson asked us to take care of his wife back home, who was pregnant, and he talked to us about our mission. Doc gave him an injection of morphine for the pain, but it didn't knock him out; he somehow remained conscious. We were under attack the entire time we waited for the medical evacuation helicopter to arrive—almost fifty minutes.

It was the worst thing I ever witnessed.

A few hours later, after the sun had set, I was on my shift as radio watch, back at Patrol Base (PB) Beatley, listening to information as it came in from the Marines who were outside of the wire. During the silence of breaks in radio traffic I couldn't help but let my mind wander back to the hours before. Was Stinson still alive? How would his wife and family handle the news? Would I be able to survive something like that if, or when, it happened to me? As my brain raced to compartmentalize the recent past, my present reality suddenly became even worse.

Loose dirt crumbled out of cracks in the walls as the room shook; a second later, the sound of a massive explosion reached us. More than a mile away, Lance Corporal Dakota Huse had been making his way through dark fields and tree lines with his squad on night patrol; they were moving toward a village to our south. The Taliban would flood fields in order to make it harder for us to advance quickly. The inundated fields didn't slow down our tall guys much, because the water was only about as high as their boots; but for shorter guys, like Dakota and me, the water was up to our ankles and even our calves at times. Between the water, our 22-pound Squad Automatic Weapon (SAW), 20 to 30 pounds of machine-gun ammo, and 45 pounds of gear, it was hard to move quickly. And the Taliban knew that.

As Huse and his squad approached the village, he reached a goat path—a small trail that surrounds an agricultural field and allows locals to travel through the patchwork of land without damaging their crops. Stepping onto it a few moments later, nineteen-year-old Dakota, from Greenwood, Louisiana, took his last step and breath on this earth.

We had no idea what the next two weeks had in store for us.

Ten days later, word came from command that we needed to expand our area of operation to create more of a presence in the area. My squad got orders to help establish a new compound in a village to the south—the same one where Huse had stepped on the IED—because it was a Taliban stronghold in the region. It was late afternoon, and we packed up our gear to start our push from Patrol Base Beatley toward the village as soon as the sun started to set. The walk was only about two clicks (kilometers), but it was better to do it at night because the Taliban rarely attack when it's dark; they know we have night-vision capability.

Second squad had found a house with a fairly good vantage point when they had patrolled the area earlier, and our job was to take that building and use it for observing the village and as a home base as we sent out patrols. Whenever that happened, we had vouchers we would give to the occupants, which they would take to the nearest FOB (forward operating base) in the area, where they would get paid for the use of their building. Our move there was uneventful, though the people in the home were reluctant to leave at first, which is understandable. But eventually they accepted the extremely generous voucher and cleared out so we could set up. We named every patrol base after someone who had been killed, but since there was already a PB Jackson elsewhere in Afghanistan, we dubbed the house PB Dakota, in honor of our friend who had died just days earlier. (For a satellite image of PB Dakota, see page 7 of the photo insert.)

The village compound was tiny—no bigger than a hotel conference room—and the home we were occupying was only two stories high, though it was one of the largest structures in the area. Unfortunately, the intel we had received proved accurate: There were Taliban in the village, and they weren't happy about our arrival and choice of landing spot.

As we unpacked our gear for the night, Nick Eufrazio and I chatted a bit about what might be waiting for us at this outpost. Nick was one of my best friends, even though we couldn't have been any more different. He was from Plymouth, Massachusetts, and cursed like a sailor; I was a Southern boy who had grown up going on church youth group mission trips. That's part of why I thought Nick was so great: He was my complete opposite, but he was fiercely loyal. He was the youngest guy on our squad, yet he also was one of the most respected. Nick didn't care whether you looked like him, sounded like him, thought like him; it didn't matter if you cheered for the Patriots and the Red Sox or the Falcons and the Braves—he was going to have your back no matter what. In high school, he had been a part of the Young Marine program, and his singular goal in life was to become a "Mustang"—that is, to be selected for Officer Candidate School from the enlisted ranks. He was the first to volunteer for the tasks no one wanted, like manning a checkpoint for locals, and he always did it with enthusiasm. His trademark gesture was a little thumbs-up. It was a simple gesture, but always accompanied by a smile. When Nick gave you a thumbs-up, you knew he was already on top of whatever you were asking from him. Every day, his attitude and outlook inspired me to be a little better, too—not just a better Marine, but a better person. His example encouraged me not just to have the cleanest weapon and heaviest pack; he was the sort of person who made you want to attack your day and life.

The next day, when it was my turn to stand post on the roof—that is, to scan the surrounding landscape and buildings for any enemy activity—an enemy sniper started firing on my position, with me in his crosshairs. The rest of the guys on the ground floor were scrambling to fill sandbags and toss them up so I could continue stacking them to build a protective wall around me while I laid down, manning my Squad Automatic Weapon, a light machine gun. It was the worst kind of multitasking. We were short on sandbags and the helicopter supply drop that was supposed to be delivering more supplies for us had been delayed, so we had to make do with what we had. Usually, the enemy tended to be pretty terrible shots. I don't know if it was the fact that they were using Cold War–era weapons left over from the Soviet invasion in 1979, or because many of them were goat herders and poppy farmers rather than formally trained soldiers.

But the sniper didn't let up, and unfortunately for me, he happened to be the rare skilled shot among the Taliban. Although I was able to build a small barricade on the roof without getting hit, each time he fired a round, I could feel a *thud* where the bullet struck the sandbags I was lying behind. As the afternoon sunlight started to fade, I was instructed to get off the roof and keep post in the room directly below. I gouged out a little hole in the wall so I could have a better vantage point, and about forty-five seconds later, a rocket came barreling into the roof and the sandbag wall I'd just built, completely obliterating the post position.

It was as if I had stepped into the middle of a tornado. The debris cloud surrounding me was so thick that I couldn't see and couldn't breathe.

My squad members immediately realized what had happened to the roof, and Doc Frend was scrambling for his medic bag, ready to rush in to see if there were any signs of life. Somehow, I wasn't injured and was able to get up and walk out of the room on my own. To hear my buddies describe the scene, no one realized I was alive until I appeared like Chuck Norris, strolling out without a scratch from an epic cloud of war. Never mind that my ears were still ringing and I was seeing double—it was better the way they told it.

As I stumbled out of the building, I muttered a few choice words to myself as I thought of all the sandbags we'd just lost and all the bullets I had dodged trying to build a wall that had pretty much been vaporized. It wasn't until later that I realized how mentally wrong that reaction was. I should have been glad that I hadn't been up there when the rocket came in rather than mad my work had been for naught.

After a big show like the rocket attack, I guess the enemy decided to take it easy for the rest of the afternoon. Later that night, at around midnight, while another Marine was on post, the roof collapsed from the damage done by the rocket earlier that day. He was fine, but we had officially lost the roof as a vantage point.

From this post we were facing four major challenges. The first was that we had previously had two positions in the compound on each of the two roofs, but now we only had one, so we had to double up on the remaining roof. The second was that it wasn't a great position to begin with, since we couldn't see as far out as we would have liked from just two stories up. The third was that we were now dangerously low on sandbags. And the fourth was that, because we only had enough sandbags for a three- or four-foot stack, we would have to stand post in a somewhat reclined position in order not to be exposed. That limited our vantage even more because we could not see directly over the edge of the building without showing ourselves, so we couldn't constantly monitor the immediate perimeter. That meant the enemy could sneak up right alongside the building, throw an explosive over the compound wall or fire at us, and then dart away into the interwoven dirt compounds throughout the village before we even spotted them. This was less than ideal. But then again, war in general is a less than ideal situation, so we're talking about degrees between awful and horrendous.

The weakness of our position was proved almost immediately. We heard a little *thud, thud, thud* from the courtyard outside the building, as if someone were tossing something over the compound wall. There was just enough time to ask "Who's throwing rocks?" before the first round of explosions began. They weren't rocks, they were grenades. Brad Skipper had been sitting outside as he cleaned his weapon, and as he took off running for cover, a grenade exploded near him. He staggered into the house, squirting blood from a hole in his spleen.

I had been outside in the courtyard of the compound helping dig a burn pit and fill more sandbags. When I saw what happened, I took off after Skipper, reaching the house just a few seconds after him. Doc, who was inside, stuck his finger into Skipper's wound to stop the bleeding while he grabbed his supplies. Skipper kept pounding on his chest to tell us he couldn't breathe. I kneeled down next to his head, assuring him he was going to be okay, and that pretty soon he'd have all the ice cream he could eat in the hospital. Doc grabbed what he needed and performed a needle thoracentesis on Skipper for a collapsed lung. It was the first one he had ever performed. I cringed watching him jam a needle into Skipper's side. But when we heard what sounded like a balloon letting out air as Skipper's reinflated lung exhaled, we all wanted to high-five Doc.

But he was a little busy. Jake Belote, who had also been outside in the courtyard, had made his way into the house as well, white as a sheet and covered in blood from where shrapnel had hit him in the groin.

Two things were abundantly clear to me: Corpsmen are worth their weight in gold, and PB Dakota was not going to be held easily.

Everything I've shared so far took place in a twenty-four-hour window in a tiny map-dot deep in the bowels of Helmand Province, Afghanistan. It was days like this that made me indifferent to the gunfire when I woke up on the morning of November 21, 2010. I unzipped my sleeping bag and thought, *Here we go again. Another day in Afghanistan.*

Firing had started when the sun came up, and we already knew what kind of day it was going to be: AK-47s shooting at us and probably a few more grenades and rockets. Great.

It was a Sunday, and if I had still been in school, we would have been on Thanksgiving break. I took my time rolling out of my sleeping bag; I'd have moved a lot faster if my mom had been calling me down for breakfast. Somehow, a packet of dehydrated beef or whatever else was left in the MRE (Meal, Ready-to-Eat) stash didn't motivate me in quite the same way.

The good news was that our solution to the visibility problem on post was that we were going to put two people on the roof at the same time. This gave us an extra set of eyes to help evaluate the scene. It also meant someone to talk to instead of four hours alone, just staring out at the desolate village and wondering if each breath you took would be your last. It's easy to get lost in your own head when you stand post alone.

Nick and I began our shift at noon. It was quiet—almost eerily so—during the entire four-hour shift. Because there were so few sandbags, it was most comfortable to lean back against them and then turn to look out. As we scanned the weirdly silent village, waiting for something to pop off at any second, we went through the different scenarios we might encounter: "Okay, if we get attacked from this direction, you do this and I'll do this. But if it's from the other direction, we'll need to do this instead."

I was glad to be on post with Nick—especially on that day, when something just felt off.

It was too quiet, given what the last few days had been like, so I told Nick I was going to see about getting us another weapon. The fighting usually went in cycles during the day, and we were just getting to the time when the Taliban usually increased their attacks. Even though things were calm right now, I didn't want to be stranded up there in a fairly exposed position without time to reload our weapons in a firefight. I went down to the room below and asked Doc if I could borrow his M-4. Our squad leader, Sergeant Rudy Najera, told me, "Don't take Doc's weapon; he might need it. Take mine." I grabbed it and hurried back up to the roof to our luxurious "recliners"—the sandbags that were awkwardly holding us halfway up.

Nick and I started going over the "What if?" scenarios again. We hadn't seen any grenades our entire deployment—that is, until the day before. Previously the enemy preferred guns and rockets. But after seeing grenades thrown over the walls of the compound yesterday, we now knew they were a possibility.

"So, Nick," I joked, making fun of his crazy-strong Massachusetts accent as best I could. "What happens if they throw a grenade up here?"

"My ass is off this f——ing roof," he said.

I laughed. "Dude, I'm right behind you."

Chapter 2
It Starts at Home

My dad will tell you that I had more confidence than any other little kid in history. When I was still a toddler, I insisted he draw the Superman logo on my chest with a marker—and not some weak, washable marker that would come off in the bathtub. No, I had to be the Man of Steel in *permanent* marker, and I wanted the logo redrawn every time the ink started to fade.

Aside from my secret superhero identity, I was exactly like every other little boy in Mississippi. I was fearless, restless, reckless, relentless—a tiny blond ball of energy who climbed up, leapt from, played on, rolled in, ran around, or found a way to destroy whatever I possibly could. And my dad and mom were thrilled about it. Truly.

From the start, my parents, Jim and Robin, taught me to believe in myself. Of course they protected me and worried about me at times, but they also made me believe that anything was possible. They had both grown up in wonderfully stable and loving homes that had also been a little bit sheltered. My mom had set a goal to make sure her kids expanded their horizons. My dad made sure he didn't just spend time with his kids, but *quality* time with them, engaging with us in meaningful and deeply personal ways. Both of them hit their parenting goals squarely on the head.

Before I was old enough for school, my mom and I used to go on daylong car trips, exploring every back road and pit stop within a tank of gas from our home just outside of Jackson. My mom's sisters all lived within a few hours' drive, so I was often playing with cousins if I wasn't out exploring the world with my mom. Dad would come home from work at six and put his hand on the hood of Mom's car as he walked in the house; almost inevitably, it would still be warm from whatever all-day adventure had kept us out until just a few minutes earlier. We even made a game of it: Dad would walk in and ask what we had done that day, and I would shrug innocently and say, "Nothing. We just stayed at home." Then I would start cracking up and we'd tell him all about our latest escapade over dinner. Dad said we were like a couple of teenage buddies with an obsession for road trips. Mom just figured that the world was for exploring—new experiences, new people, new perspectives—and we might as well do it together.

My dad indulged my fearless side by helping me build bike ramps while I was still in kindergarten so that I could practice jumps and stunts and whatever else made me feel invincible. Skinned knees and bruised shins heal, he reasoned, but forging an inner confidence would last forever. We would talk while we worked, about anything and everything, so that our construction projects were also exercises in philosophy, religion . . . and whatever Transformers I was currently into. He also sat with me for hours while I made him blow hundreds of gum bubbles until I had figured out how to do it myself. I had a stubborn sense of competition; if there was something I wanted to figure out, I was relentless until I mastered it. This trait would become one of my defining characteristics. Later in life it would prove essential; as a little kid, I imagine it was probably just annoying.

I desperately wanted siblings, but that proved a particularly elusive goal marked with a lot of loss. The hardest was a stillborn baby boy when I was four. I had been over the moon about getting a little brother and crushed when it didn't happen, but you can imagine how devastated my parents were. To lose a child and feel completely powerless as it is happening has got to be one of life's greatest agonies.

Finally, two months after my sixth birthday, my mom gave birth to twin boys they named Price and Peyton, and I was smitten. I could not imagine anything in the world more special than getting *two* siblings at once. I could not have been prouder. These weird, squirmy, pinkish bundles would be my best friends, the ones I would share secrets with and build forts with and wrestle with and get in trouble with and help get *out* of trouble when they needed it. I couldn't wait to play with them, which inevitably led to torturing them (which I will maintain to my last breath is any older sibling's birthright).

And I did mess with them. We had a hideous purplish van nicknamed "the Raisin," and I would sit in the very back row with my two little brothers in front of me, and somehow I came up with a weird breathing sound that I could do right behind them. It drove them absolutely crazy. Sometimes I'd say their names while doing it, so that it was a creepy sound right next to their ears—but Mom and Dad couldn't hear a thing. Price and Peyton would spin around and try to smack me or tell on me for messing with them, and I would pretend to be totally innocent while my brothers got in trouble for acting out.

My brothers got more fun as they got older. They were both tough little guys, so I sometimes didn't mind when they tagged along with my friends and me. I was proud of what good athletes they were, but when we played football with the neighborhood kids and an older boy kept knocking them down way harder than necessary, I would tell him to lay off and even get in a bit of a scuffle. *I* could mess with my brothers, but no one else could.

I was obsessed with any kind of physical challenge, so sports became a major part of my childhood. Aside from the birth of my brothers, the thing I was most proud of was making the Brandon All Stars in Brandon, Mississippi, when I was in first grade. It was a coach-pitched baseball league, and my dad was usually the one throwing the balls. I lived for those games. Even getting dressed for them was an elaborate ritual. My parents still tease me to this day about how long it took me to make sure that the stripes on my socks were perfectly straight, my sweatband placed exactly right, my wrists taped just like the pros'. Dad swears I was the only kid my age and size he's ever met with an actual swagger. When I was ready to play, nothing in the world could have convinced me I was anything short of the entire Atlanta Braves' starting lineup rolled into one.

Unfortunately, I got to play for the Brandon All Stars, and wear their amazing striped socks, for only one season. My dad worked in sales management in the poultry industry, and as he moved up the chain, we moved among the plants. We relocated several times within Mississippi when I was little, and then he switched companies when I was in second grade. We lived in Gainesville, Georgia, for seven years before moving to Savannah, Tennessee, located in the southwest corner of the state.

I started eighth grade there and loved every minute of it. I had a wonderful group of friends in the neighborhood, a great church, and a youth group I rarely missed week to week. Every summer we would go on mission trips to work in different communities and meet people from various walks of life, and every summer I would come home with a new sense of perspective and gratefulness for the safe, stable home my parents provided.

On one of those summer youth group trips, when I was about twelve, we ended up at a thrift store for some reason, and I found a gray T-shirt with MARINES written across the chest in black letters. There was nothing fancy about it, but that shirt became the most prized article of clothing I owned since my first-grade baseball uniform. I wore it everywhere. Something about what it represented captured my imagination. Never mind that I had no actual ties to the Marine Corps; it was the middle-school version of the Superman logo my dad used to draw on my chest.

By the time eighth grade was wrapping up, I had a singular goal in life: to earn a starting spot on the high school football team by the beginning of my junior year. Ours was a 4A school in Tennessee—a small one, granted, but a 4A school all the same—which meant that this was a pretty ambitious dream because while the level of competition was big, I was not. My mom is five-two, and I inherited my height from her—just a few inches taller. But that competitive streak within me kicked into high gear, and I could think of nothing else but pushing myself to make that dream a reality. I was a lot smaller than most of the other guys, and I didn't know if I could count on a growth spurt to boost my chances, so I kept working to make up what I lacked in size with speed and skill.

Finally, as the summer practices between my sophomore and junior years came to a close and the starting lineup was posted on the door of the football field house, there was my name: KYLE CARPENTER—STRONG SAFETY.

I had done it. I had accomplished the thing I had dedicated the last three years of my life to pursuing. It was elating—and also incredibly deflating. We'd just learned that my family was moving to South Carolina in a matter of weeks.

My parents have often remarked to me that one of the things that stood out to them most in my childhood was my tendency to pull people in. I could walk into a room and immediately detect the person there who most needed a friend, and I would fill that role. I never thought about it consciously; I just did it automatically. I guess I've just always been partial to the underdog, maybe because I could always feel people underestimating me because of my size. Helping someone be recognized for who they are and who they can be is exciting for me. I love being a fan and helping other people discover whatever or whomever I'm excited about, too. It seems like the simplest gift you can give someone, but one of the best: to make them know they are seen.

I had never fully appreciated what that could do for someone until we moved to a tiny town just outside of Lexington, South Carolina, and I was suddenly dropped into the middle of an enormous high school that served the entire county. The graduating classes were between nine hundred and a thousand students, and I went from being a football stud to a nobody. Now I was the person hoping someone would notice me.

My dad and I went out to South Carolina a few weeks ahead of my mom and brothers so that I could be there in time for football camp at my new school, but the experience was disheartening. I did all right the first couple of practices. I showed I was fast and could catch well, but beyond that, what did the coaches and the other guys care about me? No one knew who I was. They hadn't seen evidence of how disciplined I could be about mastering a skill. The reputation I'd worked so hard to cultivate with my coaches back in Savannah meant nothing here: a guy who would always show up ready for practice and give 100 percent; someone who didn't get into fights or get put on academic probation. No one knew how hard I had worked or how dedicated I had been over the past few years to develop as a leader. Basically, no one at my new school knew my character. It wasn't anyone's fault; it was just the way the chips fell. I was starting from scratch as a guy weighing 135 pounds, trying out for football at one of the largest high schools in the state.

I'm rarely someone who gives up, but at that moment, I just couldn't see the point. It wasn't worth it to me to continue making it my life's mission to earn a starting spot on a team where none of the coaches even knew my name. I've always been an optimist, but that doesn't mean you can't be a realist, too. Realistically, I knew I would graduate before I ever saw the field earlier than the fourth quarter. So I quit. And the months following that decision remain, to this day, one of the lowest periods of my life. I hadn't just lost. I had given up—the opposite of who I was. For the first time ever in my life, I felt like I didn't have a purpose. Every other move we made had felt like an adventure, never a loss, because my parents worked so hard to ensure we felt stable at home; but this move just felt different. I would go back to the hotel where we were staying until our house was ready, and I would cry for what felt like hours because I had never felt so devoid of joy, of life, of community, of goals, of hope. Maybe that sounds like an overly dramatic response to quitting a sport, but there was so much more bound up in that choice for me than just hanging up my cleats.

The school year started at Lexington High, and I was relieved to find that, as big as the school was, I could not have asked for a nicer crowd of people to be there with me. I made some fantastic friends who helped make the school feel a little smaller and a little less intimidating, but there was still something missing. There was a hole in my heart for the feeling of belonging that I had left behind in Tennessee.

On New Year's Day, after my dad had gotten home from work, my parents sat me down for a talk. Dad cleared his throat and said, with a note of apology in his voice, "I know you're unhappy at Lexington."

I shrugged. Four months ago I would have said, "Yes, sir," but I didn't really feel like myself anymore.

Dad pushed on. "If you are interested, there is a small, 1A private school out in the middle of nowhere, about thirty minutes away, near where I work. What would you think about giving it a visit?"

I shrugged again: "Sure." I wasn't familiar with the school he was talking about, but I was willing to try anything.

So when the new semester started in January, I moved from the gargantuan, multistory county high school to begin at W. Wyman King Academy, a tiny, K–12 Christian school where I had fewer than twenty-five students in the junior class with me—and that was one of the biggest classes they'd ever had.

It immediately felt like home.

The sense of community I had been missing was there in those cinder-block walls. Within a few weeks, when baseball season started, I knew I was returning to myself, climbing out of the pit where I'd felt stuck; I was a person with a niche and a purpose once again. King Academy proved to be exactly the kind of environment I needed at precisely that time in my life. I may have been the new kid who just transferred in, but it felt as if there was already a place for me there.

I think my parents really knew I was back when I started hanging around with "Dirt Road," the nickname I gave to a tall, gangly country boy who went to King but always seemed a little unsure of where he fit in. I got a kick out of his goofy sense of humor and his wholehearted dedication to whatever he was into at the moment. Even as I was trying to make inroads with the social groups that were already established, I decided to bring Dirt Road along with me so that we could find our footing together. From my parents' point of view, if I was back to drawing people out of the shadows and into a group of friends, I was back to being Kyle. And they were right. I could feel myself fitting in comfortably, like the tumblers in a lock falling around a key. I still missed my friends in Tennessee, but I wasn't questioning who I was or what I was doing. I now had an even greater understanding of what it felt like to be an outsider without a sense of belonging.

I loved the guest speakers who visited the school. That was an important part of our curriculum, listening to men and women share fascinating stories about their own struggles and successes that shaped their character. The one who had the greatest impact on me was a Vietnam veteran named Clebe McClary. While serving in the Marines in 1968, Clebe took heavy shrapnel from a grenade that cost him his left eye and his left arm at the elbow. Now, he and his wife run a nonprofit focused on helping military families navigate the stresses and challenges of deployment and combat injuries. At the time, I wasn't as taken with the fact that he had been a Marine or wounded in battle as I was with the fact that he was someone who really understood how to live. Despite his advancing age and his significant injuries, he was still active, engaged, and dynamic. If ever there was someone who had an excuse to throw in the towel, it was Clebe—but he didn't. I was in awe of his spirit—that someone who had been through so much could create an incredible life not only in spite of, but *because* of his experiences.

I told my parents all about Clebe McClary after that presentation, and how I couldn't imagine rebuilding a life after something as devastating as what he went through. I realized, as a teenager, I had no idea what life was going to throw at me, but I knew that I wanted to meet whatever challenges came my way with the same grace, determination, and passion as Clebe. At the time, I couldn't foresee when or how I would end up applying the lessons he shared and the example he offered, but I understood I had just witnessed a special man and a special way of living.

There was one more thing about King that really helped me recapture my confidence: They had a football team. The school's coach, an amazing man named Jolly Doolittle, was a bit of a legend. Coach Doolittle was a great teacher who was really funny with the students, but who would also absolutely destroy you on the field in practice. He knew how to push you beyond what you thought possible, so that you ended up capable of stuff you had never imagined you could do. Because the squad was small—only about fifteen to twenty guys—I was on the field for everything except for kickoff team. On offense I was a running back, and on defense I played corner. Fourth-quarter cramps were inevitable, and by the end of every game I was completely gassed. But I finished the season with over 2,200 yards in offense, more than 20 touchdowns, and 3 kickoff returns for touchdowns. It was a different kind of game from playing at a big school, but I loved it. In fact, the year I was able to play for King Academy, my senior year, we went to the state championships, losing in the finals in double overtime.

It was a heartbreaking end to the season, but it was wonderful to know my family was up in the stands, cheering us on, every single play. And they didn't just show up for the big games, like the state championship; my parents worked hard to make sure they were present for every school activity and game they could possibly make for my brothers and me. I know it was hard with their jobs to be able to rearrange their schedules to accommodate the extracurriculars of three active boys, but they found a way to make it happen. It made a big difference for Price, Peyton, and me in terms of how supported we felt. There was never a sense that we were alone or unimportant; we always knew our family would be our biggest fans and the loudest cheering section, whatever we had going on.

When I reflect now on my life growing up, I am amazed at how fortunate I was to grow up in the home I did. I never knew what it was like *not* to have the complete, unwavering support of my parents. That didn't mean they didn't discipline me or that they always took my side. But I never questioned if they were acting in my best interest. I never had to wonder if they were going to be all in for me.

The example my parents set was instrumental in shaping who I became and how I engaged the world. Everything in our home was about developing character, humility, and resilience. My parents focused on raising my brothers and me to be functional, rational, contributing members of society; even as they let us enjoy amazing childhoods, they always had an eye on what sort of adults they wanted us to become. Chore charts and church trips were a given. We were expected to take responsibility for making the house run smoothly, and we were encouraged to be involved with our community. Life was about more than what we could take out of it; it was about making a difference—not necessarily on some global scale, but by improving someone's day or helping to lift someone up.

I realize there are many people out there who weren't fortunate enough to have the kind of stable, loving parents that I was blessed with, which is why I don't take my family for granted. There is something to be said for the so-called all-American childhood: respect your father, love your mama, stick tight to your brothers, always do your best, always be honest, and never talk back. Like any family, ours wasn't perfect, but it absolutely gave me the foundation I needed to become the adult I wanted to be. As the saying goes, my parents gave me "roots and wings"—and none of us had any idea how important both those gifts would prove to be.

Chapter 3
Hard Work Pays Off

My parents did not believe in shortcuts, and I always claimed I believed the same thing . . . until I was eighteen and my dad got me a job at the chicken-processing plant where he worked. I figured I would be some kind of an errand boy, starting the coffee in the mornings, maybe filing some paperwork or answering phones in the air-conditioned office. Dad didn't pull any strings, though, and I was definitely *not* the boss's son; I was Kyle-the-new-hire. My first day, I went in feeling pretty full of myself. Just saying, "I'm going to work," had such a grown-up, important sound to it. That feeling lasted all of thirty seconds. True, there was a little filing and organizing, but there was a whole lot more manual labor: I swept floors, I checked the temperature of the birds, I did quality-assurance checks, I unloaded chickens from their truck onto the back dock, and I hosed out chicken containers. I can assure you, it is impossible to feel full of yourself when you're dealing with chicken poop, stray feathers, and hard-on-the-hands work.

I dreaded heading into work each day. The sights, sounds, and smells of any animal-processing facility are more than enough for a teenager to get used to. But that's the reality of the large-scale animal farming industry across the United States, which feeds the nation as well as many people around the world. And it's important to note that in poultry-processing facilities, fully one-third of the day is spent sanitizing every inch of the plant.

There are so many aspects of a chicken plant that are different from your average nine-to-five job. Besides the sanitizing, there are a number of other precautions you have to take. If you are going to be anywhere on the processing floor, you have to wear rubber shoe covers or boots, hair and beard nets, safety goggles, a uniform overcoat, gloves, and hearing protection. One of the other most important aspects of working with chicken at a processing plant is making sure that the birds aren't stressed: a panicked chicken releases lactic acid into its system, which pools in the muscles and causes tougher cuts of meat; also, it's just more humane for the birds to be kept as calm as possible. As a result, in the room where the live chickens are loaded onto the line, the only light source is one red bulb. This helps make the birds a little more relaxed and calm. It is a pretty small space and with the darkness broken by only one or two red light bulbs, it actually looks a lot like an old-school darkroom or the inside of a nuclear sub—either would have been preferable to me.

If I worked the morning shift, from seven to three, I'd peek in before I left at Price and Peyton sleeping in, carefree twelve-year-olds on summer break, and think, *You have no idea how good you have it right now.* If I worked second shift, I'd get home late at night, exhausted, and with the scent of hard work clinging to every hair and every inch of skin on my body. After each shift, I would scrub it off as best I could in the shower, and then stare at my brothers running around, full of energy or complaining about some little thing, and in all my eighteen years of wisdom I would shake my head and think, *Just you wait a few summers until Dad makes y'all do this, too.*

As awful as I thought that job was, I developed a whole new appreciation for not only the value but also the importance of hard work. I had always been taught that the way you apply yourself to your job is a reflection of your character, and my parents were insistent that there is no such thing as being "too good" for any kind of honest employment. But my time at the poultry-processing facility forced me to appreciate the real, and often "invisible," work that people do to deliver food to grocery stores and dinner tables. Many of us think our food comes from the grocery store. I can assure you it does not. It was sobering for me to realize firsthand how many hardworking people do a job that allows us to grab food at a store without giving a second thought to how it got there.

I didn't enjoy the work, but I did love the people and the satisfying exhaustion at the end of each day. It reminded me of when I played sports, how tired I felt after a long practice. I loved the perspective it gave me working alongside people I might never have met otherwise. And truth be known, I loved knowing that the summer job was eventually going to end.

I also gained an important mentor in my supervisor, Rodney Taylor. He was in charge of sanitation for the plant, and a leader like none I had ever met before. He was rough around the edges, authentic. He rolled up his sleeves and worked alongside his team whenever an extra set of hands was needed; he wasn't above grime or hard work. Since workers at the plant were from various walks of life, he learned to relate to his people in order to be able to communicate effectively with them rather than getting frustrated at the differences in everyone's backgrounds. He believed that his workers would respect him more if he was able to connect with them directly. He also believed that they could do their own jobs more efficiently if they weren't afraid to ask him for clarification. He regularly checked in with all of us to see how things were going in our lives and how we were doing. If someone made a mistake, there was just as much focus on fixing the problem or gaining a new skill or knowledge as there was on the mistake itself. If something needed doing, he was there doing it or willing to help whoever was. The harder the job, the more it seemed to energize him. He was also the most creative swearer I'd ever met, and to any teenage boy, no matter how straitlaced, that is impressive. Most inspiring to me, though, was the fact that he always put himself second and made sure that his workers were taken care of first.

This message had been reinforced at school. Since King Academy was so small, we didn't have a full-time groundskeeper who kept the grass on our football field meticulously mowed or the baseball diamond groomed to perfection. Instead, the upkeep of our facilities fell to the team, and it proved to be one of the most mean- ingful aspects of my education. Prepping our fields was part of our pre- and in-season training and team bonding to get ourselves and our field into shape for competition. There is a different kind of pride you take in something that demands so much sweat equity and personal sacrifice. We were deeply proud of the way the diamond looked after months of raking rocks out of the infield and rolling out the fence ourselves. We knew firsthand what it took to prepare and maintain what we had, and we treated our fields, stands, and buildings with a kind of reverence. The summer before my senior year, the football team took on the construction of a new field house/concession stand/ press box. The school secured all the permits and had qualified builders on-site, but it was us, the players, who hauled the materials, mixed the mortar, stacked the cinder blocks, framed the doors, mounted hinges, and painted. The sense of accomplishment from creating something out of nothing was incredible. The structure would outlast us and serve the school long after we had graduated. It gave the season a new significance.

That satisfaction in a job well done was also part of my fierce competition with myself; I never wanted to avoid doing whatever it took to get better or do better, and that meant putting in the required work. It also meant not being afraid of being challenged. Take baseball, for instance. I had to practice hard to be passably below average, but I was determined to get better. I might work on hitting for months and only see a slight boost in my stats, but that was enough to make me keep pushing, even if I was frustrated or exhausted. I know this will break my dad's heart (he truly loves the game), but baseball was just an enjoyable way for me to pass time until football season started. It kept me hungry and humble while I pushed through. I liked the fact that baseball made me chase skills that didn't come naturally to me. It forced me to develop discipline and stick with something even when I knew I wasn't going to come out as MVP.

Football, on the other hand, lit my passion. I loved that I could see a direct correlation between the amount of time I spent practicing and the results on the field. If I was trying to cut a ninety-degree corner while running at full speed, I knew that if I dedicated hours on the field, by the time the lights came on in the evening, I would be a whole lot closer to having mastered the skill than I had been that morning. I used everything as fuel, now that I think about it—both the challenge *and* the reward. If something eluded me, I pursued it exhaustively until I figured it out. If something came fairly easily, I kept at it until I excelled. I know perfection is impossible, but I always felt like it should still be the goal.

There's probably no better example of this than weight-lifting my senior year. I weighed less than 140 pounds at the time, but I kept pushing myself in training in an attempt to pass 405 pounds in squat presses. I relished pushing the boundaries not only of what people imagined someone my size could do, but also . . . well, pushing the laws of physics. Once you get up to four 45-pound weights on each side of the 45-pound bar, you actually have to switch to a thicker, more durable bar. The idea of having maxed out the standard capacity of a weight-lifting bar was thrilling. A big part of what drove me to do that was the reassurance and boost of confidence from my coaches and teammates each time I went up in weight. It was affirming to have people cheering me on as I continued to go beyond what anyone expected. Every time I was in the weight room I pushed myself as hard as I possibly could, but I was also encouraged and uplifted by smaller guys who would tell me, "I hope to squat that much one day." I felt like even though my goal was a personal one, people joined me because they felt motivated, too, seeing someone tenaciously inching toward an unlikely achievement. As I kept pushing, I found that I didn't feel shame if I didn't make the goal I'd set for the day; I knew I just had to keep working and keep suffering. That suffering paid off. Thanks to that stubbornness and the adrenaline of competition, my senior year I placed first in the state for speed and strength in my weight class, benching 215, power cleaning 225, and squatting 425 pounds. To say I was proud doesn't do it justice—I was ecstatic. I had fought for every single pound, and the blood, sweat, and tears I invested in that championship were all worth it in that moment.

It wasn't an obsession—I didn't eat, sleep, and breathe my goals or feel devastated if I didn't reach them. It was more like a healthy lack of complacency. Curiosity about my own limits drove me and motivated me. Discomfort was temporary; I knew that practice would be over in a few hours, or the manual labor at the chicken plant would end when school started. There was something emboldening in knowing that I had stuck it out rather than quitting when things were difficult, unpleasant, or seemed impossible. I never wanted to walk away from something knowing that I could have done more or tried a little bit harder. Even if that extra bit of effort didn't change the outcome at all, at least I would know that I threw everything I had at it. No one could ever say I was a quitter.

As important as the positive experiences were— when I performed well, maximized my natural talents, or made a big impact in competition—it was the more difficult moments that really shaped my character. The work in the chicken factory proved to me that I could endure more than I thought and that there was real dignity and deep satisfaction in hard, manual labor; it also showed me that a willingness to try something completely different could broaden my horizons and introduce me to new people and perspectives. Even though I didn't realize it at the time, my willingness to keep slogging away at baseball taught me to appreciate more the things that came easily; the work/reward imbalance and the stick-to-it-iveness required to keep at a sport that was never going to love me back helped me develop some serious grit that would serve me well later in life.

In the end, I think what it came down to was the fact that I thrived on challenge. I had been raised to believe that anything was possible and I hated feeling like there might be something out there that could beat me. Part of it, I know, was being young and believing I was invincible; I had never yet met something I couldn't conquer with enough time and energy or that I couldn't bounce back from with enough tenacity. Maybe that Sharpie marker my dad used to draw the Superman *S* on my chest never fully washed off. Maybe it was watching guys like Rodney Taylor and recognizing that there was something in the way that he carried himself that he obviously hadn't learned by taking the easy road.

All I knew was that I wasn't ready to sit in more classrooms. Not yet. As my friends started talking about college and doing campus visits, I found myself thinking about what could challenge me more than anything else had up to that point. College could wait, but I wasn't going to be young and in peak physical form forever. The military started to creep into my mind. And I knew that if I went that route, there was only one branch of the service that would push me as hard and challenge me as much as I hoped.

Chapter 4
Keep Your Promises—to Others *and* to Yourself

MY SENIOR YEAR OF HIGH SCHOOL: 2007–08

Most headlines were fixed on the war in Iraq, as Operation Iraqi Freedom (OIF) had been under way for almost half a decade in one form or another. In January 2007, President Bush gave a televised speech about the need for an additional 21,500 troops in the country, a move dubbed "A New Way Forward." Saddam Hussein was captured in December 2003 and executed in 2006, but the power vacuum led to increased sectarian violence. Still, seeing the images of men and women voting in the first free parliamentary elections in 2005 stirred something in me, as I think they did in most Americans. However you felt about the invasion of Iraq, those photos of people raising their inked fingers in triumph proved that progress had been made and lives were changing.

Meanwhile, in Afghanistan, there had not been nearly as much combat in the first few years after September 11, 2001, but starting in 2006, the Taliban began making significant advances and were committing atrocities against civilians in increasing numbers. It was clear that the United States was going to have to ramp up their efforts in Afghanistan if they wanted to help the Afghan people and defeat the Taliban.

Around the world, terrorist activity was increasing. From the London subway bombings in 2005 that killed 52 people and wounded almost 700 to the Mumbai train bombings in 2006 that killed nearly 200 people and injured more than 800, every time I turned on the news it seemed like the world was in chaos. War is awful and I believe it should be a last resort, but sometimes it can be the only way to restore some kind of order and help those in need. It seemed to me that the United States military had a mission to do exactly that, and I fit the bill of someone who could contribute to that effort: young, healthy, fit, willing to be challenged, and eager to be a part of something bigger than myself.

It was that last part that affected me the most. As I considered what my life might look like if I took different paths, I found myself increasingly disillusioned with the traditional, "expected" path. Everyone assumed I would go straight to college and from college right into a corporate career somewhere because that's what most clean-cut, middle-class kids with decent grades did. There is absolutely nothing wrong with that, but it didn't appeal to me. I agreed to go on campus visits with my parents to make sure I was exploring all my options, and I even met with a football coach or two at smaller schools. As much as I loved football, though, I was also a realist and I knew that my role on any college team would probably just be as a tackling dummy for four years. I didn't want to put my body through that.

But the more I looked around at colleges, the more detached I began to feel from the whole experience. I could definitely see the appeal for many people, but it wasn't where I felt I needed to be at that point in my life. I turned nineteen in October, and I had been sitting in classrooms my entire life. There were some major events in the course of human history going on in the world at that time; I wanted to get out and *do* something. In my mind, college was a choice I could make at any point in the future, but joining the military was an opportunity that would only be available to me for a handful of years while I was young. Through all of my competitions with myself when I chased after goals and challenges, I learned that I could live with pain and I could live with failure, but I absolutely could not live with regret. If I was ever going to make military service part of my life, it had to be soon—and if I missed that chance, I would never forgive myself.

One afternoon, I casually mentioned my interest in enlisting to my mother, who was not nearly as keen on it as I was. I wanted to do something that would help change the world and to learn the leadership I had seen that military service could bring; she just saw it as her son charging headlong into the most dangerous places in the world. I didn't bring the subject up again, but in my mind, I made a deal: one semester. If I liked it, I would stay and get a degree, which I knew would happen someday no matter what. If I didn't like it, I would enlist in the spring.

My parents knew I was not completely enthusiastic about college, but I think they believed that the experience of going off to school would be enough to help me shake whatever was gnawing at me.

I agreed to give college a try because I really did want to show them honor, and their blessing for my eventual enlistment was important to me. I figured I was more likely to win their support if I at least gave college a try. Ours has always been a family where respect for one another was of the highest priority, and I needed my parents to feel that I had listened to their wishes and respected them enough to legitimately take their hopes for me into consideration when making life-choices. I intended to give that semester a real shot, but I also knew, deep down, that it probably wasn't going to accomplish what they hoped it would. I felt a burning imperative to join the Marines. And I knew it was not going to be a feeling that went away; it was the only path that felt true to myself. It wasn't a matter of simply wanting adventure or fostering some idealism about changing the world—those were factors, of course—but I felt a kind of burning need to go. I was willing to postpone my plans out of respect for my parents, but I knew I could not delay them forever.

I graduated high school in the spring of 2008 and enrolled for the fall semester in a program that allows general education credits to be completed at a community college near the Clemson campus before students enroll at Clemson University. It was my first time living away from home, and I enjoyed the experience. My classmates were friendly and fun, and the classes would have been interesting if I had been able to put my heart and mind into them. The problem was that they weren't anywhere near a classroom. I couldn't bring myself simply to study concepts like basic human freedoms and democracy when there was a real and urgent need to go and actually fight for those ideals. Every time I turned on the news and saw a story about the troops in Afghanistan, my own life—heading back and forth from class, doing homework, eating in the cafeteria, sleeping in my own bed—felt shallow. I wasn't ungrateful for those things, but I felt like I was supposed to be pushing myself to do more. Theoretical discussions within classroom walls are important—it's essential to frame action with thoughtful study and thorough understanding—but those types of scholarly debates aren't real life. They are safe. Comfortable. The only real consequence of misunderstanding is a lower grade, not loss of life or limb or the instability of an entire geopolitical region for a generation. Before I could (or should) offer any real opinions on how things ought to be done, I felt like I needed to appreciate what it was like to carry out certain policies in the real world instead of questioning everything from the insulated confines of my own limited experience and perspective.

What was more, I looked around and met a lot of wonderful people in my classes, but I also saw a number of students who seemed like they were only there to party and blow through their parents' money. Of course

I realized that people like that are everywhere, but I didn't want to get pulled into that world only to look back years later and realize how much time, money, effort, opportunity, and youth I had wasted on things that didn't matter.

Halfway through the semester, I decided to visit the recruiting offices of a few different branches of the military so that my parents could see I had at least entertained service options other than the Marine Corps. I went to the Army National Guard center first, followed by a few others, but nothing else resonated with me the way the challenge and the allure of the Marines did. I don't think the Marine recruiting station I visited actually thought I was serious at first, but I was motivated and kept after them. Eventually, I went to a different Marine recruiting station and made sure that they understood that I was fully intending to enlist. I gathered all the information on the delayed-entry program, educated myself on what it would entail, and prepared to talk to my parents.

At the start of Christmas break, I took a deep breath and walked into the living room, where my father was reading in his favorite old recliner. "Dad, can I talk to you . . . on the back porch?"

He looked at me for just a moment before answering, "Sure, son," in a quiet voice.

That deck is still where all our important family discussions take place. It runs along the length of the house, overlooking the backyard and the woods, where we used to play paintball. It provides the perfect setting for serious conversations, which need to be removed from the hustle and bustle of everyday life in the house. When I told my dad I wanted to speak with him on the back porch, he had no clue what was coming—but he knew it was something serious.

I explained to him how I felt about college, and that, for the rest of my life, I wanted to be a part of a story bigger than myself. I longed to give myself to a cause that mattered. It was important to me that he understand, man-to-man, what was driving me. After we spoke for a little while, my mom joined us, and I explained my decision to her as well.

The hardest part about it all was her evident heartbreak. I knew it wasn't theatrics just to try to get me to change my mind; I could see the fear she felt for me as she begged me to consider other options. "What about the Coast Guard or the Navy or the National Guard?" she pleaded. "You can serve your country without intentionally putting yourself in the middle of active combat."

I tried to explain to her gently that I really had researched the other options, but that nothing else answered the need I was trying to meet. To her credit, she listened to me explain my reasons and point of view even as she was trying to keep her hands from shaking. When we had all said what we needed to express, we hugged and went inside.

Mom was crying, and I remember she had red eyes for most of the next two weeks. My dad was deeply concerned that my decision was stemming from a feeling of not belonging in South Carolina, and his guilt about moving us from Tennessee was more intense than ever. No amount of reassurance from me could convince him that my enlistment was not a response to my initial struggle to fit in or a reaction to any sort of deficiency in my life in South Carolina. It hurt me deeply to see that my dad felt as if he had somehow failed by pulling me away from a home, school, and friends I loved at such a crucial time in my life. I couldn't make him see that his example, the new school and friends, and everything about the way our lives had turned out were actually an important part of what was giving me the courage to attempt something bold and meaningful.

I do understand how terrifying it all had to be from my parents' point of view. We were not a family with a rich military tradition. My mom's dad had served in the Navy during the Korean War, but that was before she was born and he never talked about it afterward. We respected and celebrated the military, and wholeheartedly supported our troops, but it was a foreign world to my family, one that was particularly frightening at that moment. As bad as Iraq had been, things there were starting to quiet down as policy, attention, and resources shifted to Afghanistan; Afghanistan, meanwhile, was being described as having the potential to be worse than Iraq. That couldn't be easy news to wrap their heads around.

"This is not the plan," my mom insisted, trying to explain how this decision went against every maternal instinct she had poured into raising Price, Peyton, and me. "This is not what I had planned for you. My primary goal your whole life has been to keep you alive, and now you want to join a fighting force in the middle of a war."

My brothers' reaction could not have been any different from my parents', however. As I sat them down and explained what I was planning to do, their eyes lit up. "That's so *cool!*" Price said. Peyton joked that it basically made me a superhero. They were just a few weeks from their thirteenth birthdays, and I know they felt the tension around the house. I was grateful that my brothers were excited for me even if my parents weren't. I understood my decision would impact all of them in one way or another, and it was nice to know that my two best friends were cheering me on. What was more, I wanted to set a good example for them. Because I was six years older, I felt it was vital to show them I was standing up for my own life choices in a way that was also respectful and honoring of our family. I knew I had probably screwed up on that front a thousand times already, but this particular instance seemed too important to get wrong. It mattered to me that I set a good example in how I left the nest.

In the end, my parents saw how committed I was to my plan and how deliberate and thoughtful I had been in making it. They accepted it. They appreciated that I had talked to them first and sought their blessing, if not their permission. All three of us knew people who had enlisted behind their parents' backs.

One night, after about two weeks of going back and forth, Dad turned to Mom and said, "Robin, he's going to do this. We can either give him our blessing or not. But he's going to do this. Let's give him our blessing so we can support him."

And from that moment they were 100 percent on board.

A few months later, there was a ceremony at our church honoring veterans. The pastor talked about how the military can be a calling like any other profession. That service was important in helping my parents, at last, understand what was driving me. Dad remarked afterward, "No one just wakes up one morning and says, 'Oh, heck, I think I'll join the Marine Corps today.' Kyle thought about this and prayed about this."

Dad was exactly right: I wasn't trying to be rebellious or just seeking adventure. I felt *called* to serve.

Through that experience of delaying my enlistment out of deference for my parents' wishes, I also learned to appreciate the significance of following through on what you believe is the right path. I was an adult now, and I had put a tremendous amount of thought and research into my decision. If I had denied myself a chance to pursue my calling, I couldn't have been the person I wanted to be. I felt deeply what the right path was for my life, even though I knew it was going to be a difficult road in every imaginable way. But I also knew it was something that had impressed itself on my soul and I would never be satisfied until I attempted it. Too often, we focus on the importance of keeping our word to others while neglecting the value of keeping our word to ourselves. In the course of not wanting to let other people down or hurt them, we can end up limiting ourselves. One of the most difficult actions we can do is to gently but firmly move past someone else's outdated or imperfect idea of who we ought to be. Likewise, one of the most difficult things for someone we love is to accept that new vision of who we are. As hard as it was for my parents to let go of the specific set of plans for my life that they believed was best, I admire the fact that they eventually not only accepted but embraced and celebrated my choice.

In the coming months and years, I would come to learn what an essential part of Marine Corps leadership keeping one's word is; your fellow Marines have to be able to trust you completely, and you them. Each Marine has to know that everyone else will keep their word, otherwise you can't stay focused on the right things. Even more basic than that, however, seeing your promises through is a reflection of your character and integrity—and an essential part of integrity is respecting *yourself* enough to defend and follow through on your personal convictions.

Even as I declined to enroll in school again for the spring and instead signed my name on my enlistment papers, I knew I still owed a promise to my parents: that I would get that college degree eventually. But that was years down the road; at the moment, I had another promise to make.

In January 2009, I raised my right hand to make the Marine Corps's Oath of Enlistment. I meant every word:

I do solemnly swear that I will support and defend the Constitution of the United States against all enemies, foreign and domestic; that I will bear true faith and allegiance to the same; and that I will obey the orders of the President of the United States and the orders of the officers appointed over me, according to regulations and the Uniform Code of Military Justice. So help me God.

Chapter 5
Lead with Action

MARCH 2009

I was off to boot camp at Parris Island, South Carolina. My mom likes to say that if she had known what was to come, she would have saved up her worry. After all, boot camp was only thirteen weeks and my initial enlistment would be for four years. But good luck trying to convince my mom not to fret about something.

We had a big family send-off with lots of tears (Mom), resigned smiles (Dad), and fighting over who was going to get my room when I was gone (Price and Peyton). I found out later that my mom was feeling even more sentimental than I realized; she keeps a meticulous and exhaustive filing system for each kid, and mine includes an empty plastic bottle with a laminated label that says, "Last water bottle before Afghanistan."

Parris Island is in my home state, less than 150 miles away from my parents'. The weather was similar and the vegetation looked familiar. A long, narrow, palmetto-lined stretch of road connects the peninsula of Parris Island to the nearest town over Battery Creek (which is more like an enormous coastal inlet).

Yet Parris Island is a world apart from the rest of America. Once you get there you feel like the world just continues on without you. You don't know anything that is going on with the news, with shows on TV, or (worst of all) music and sports. You have absolutely no connection to the outside world except for one hour every Sunday when you get to write letters home.

As you near the gate of Parris Island the bus driver tells you to put your head between your legs, then you ride with your head down until the bus stops and the door opens. They do this so that if you try to run away while at boot camp you don't know which way the only exit is. It sounds crazy, but it also makes sense given what's coming next. It's got to be a universal feeling—for every Marine I've talked to, anyway—that when the door is jerked open on the bus and you step out onto the famous yellow footprints as a new recruit, you are hit with a mixture of thoughts: *Is this real? What's going on? What have I done? Oh, no. This is the beginning of a four-year obligation that I can't get out of.*

I know I absolutely had those feelings at first, but I was also determined that this was what I was supposed to be doing, so I resolved not to let anything get to me.

Easier said than done at Marine Corps boot camp.

Like any successful and efficient organization, the Marine Corps emphasizes leadership at the foundational level, with every Marine trained and ready to take over the job above them if the situation calls for it. This appealed to me as being a part of the military: the discipline that shapes recruits into leaders. Obviously, the way the Marine Corps does it is not the most pleasant approach, but it has a remarkable success rate.

Looking at my platoon photo from basic, I'm obviously the smallest guy in my class. I quickly learned that one of the biggest challenges and tests of my mental strength would be going on our hikes. I'm only five-seven with my boots on, which means that for every stride the six-four guy next to me takes, I'm taking about two. But our packs are all the same weight. We might go twelve miles carrying more than one hundred pounds of gear, so I had to work harder to stay in step than other guys. But I am hardheaded; I made it my do-or-die goal to hike until I passed out. That way, when I came to, no one could say I had decided to quit. Developing the mental toughness required to prove myself was a challenge I relished as much as I simultaneously hated it.

I was honored to be named a squad leader early on and hold that position through graduation. The drill instructors (DIs) will pick recruits who stand out to them as having special leadership qualities and give them a little bit of authority with their peers to help lead in the platoon. The DIs often cycle through a number of recruits in the first few weeks before settling on permanent squad leaders; there are usually about four of them, each watching over roughly eighteen recruits. If the DIs decide you have earned the right to stay in that role and you graduate as a squad leader, you will leave boot camp at the rank of private first class rather than private. It is an honor, but it does come with its drawbacks. You help maintain order, but you also have to share punishment with anyone in your squad who needs to be `disciplined. If one of your guys is told he has to do push-ups, you have to be there, doing them right alongside him.

That was one of the best lessons in leadership the Marine Corps taught me: A true leader is not someone who keeps themselves separate from the people they lead; he or she is right in the middle of what the team is going through, experiencing the lows as well as the highs with everyone else.

One of my drill instructors, Luke Billingsley, told me later that what impressed him most was the way I understood the importance of follow-through. If I gave an order—say, to clean the squad bay for inspection—my guys almost always fell in right away and we would complete the work together. He said they responded like that because they knew I was going to get down on my hands and knees and "scuzz" with them. (Scuzzing is a common boot camp activity that involves scrubbing or polishing the floor with a wet towel or toothbrush. Rumor has it, it was created by the devil himself.) If I gave an order, I always went back and followed up to make sure it had been completed. The point of the work was to accomplish an end goal, not simply to exercise power.

And what about the times when *I* had to be corrected (and there were more than I can count)? I tried to embrace those as lessons for future action, rather than allow myself to get down or get upset over a perceived unfairness. There were times when I got in trouble for something that one of my squad members had or had not done, and I had to be willing to accept that. Ultimately, the responsibility for the execution of any order came back to me, since I had been trusted with the job of seeing it through.

It's easy to say all this now, when I don't have a DI in my face screaming at me. Actually, what was worse than the yelling was when Billingsley would come up next to me and just whisper, "Carpenter." It was as if all the bad karma I had accrued from teasing my little brothers was now coming back on me a hundredfold. Most of your time in boot camp, you aren't called anything except "Recruit," in order to help you build your identity as part of the platoon, so hearing my name singled out by one of the most intimidating human beings I have ever met got to me. A whisper was all it took. Billingsley is not a particularly huge guy, but he has got to be one of the toughest Marines in the Corps. All he had to do was lean over and just growl my name, and I was scared straight.

Despite my best efforts, in the end, the Marine Corps did break me, just as they do everyone. What got me wasn't any exhaustive physical torture. It was a simple drill—a choreographed foot movement for marching in formation—that I couldn't seem to master. That one little step was the thing that finally put me over the edge. I was frustrated, I was hot, I was hungry, and now there was this stupid, simple thing that made my brain flip into "Marine mode."

Suddenly, I wasn't thinking about myself anymore. "I" became the platoon and the platoon became me. I wasn't Kyle Carpenter, trying to master the minutiae of inconsequential footwork. My performance on the parade deck mattered to the overall good of my platoon. One wrong step as a leader can have a ripple effect on your entire platoon. That moment of realization is hard to explain if you've never lived it, but it is an essential part of military training. It is how the tribe survives in combat. You look to the Marine to your left and right, and you know that you will one day be facing fire with them and for them, and they will do the same for you.

This point was driven home when those of us who had chosen Infantry as our military occupational specialty (MOS) were informed that a troop surge was likely coming. An influx of Marines were anticipated to be sent to Afghanistan in the next twenty-four months. In short, we definitely would be seeing combat.

By the time we got to the "Crucible," the grueling, fifty-four-hour culminating event that caps off your time at boot camp, our platoon was one unit that felt as if we were going to live or die together. Every obstacle in the Crucible is named for a different Marine who was awarded the Medal of Honor. Part of the experience is learning their stories of bravery and loyalty, and honoring the history of which we are all about to become a part as newly minted Marines. The Marine Corps's motto is *Semper Fidelis*, meaning "always faithful." I wanted to be a leader who was always faithful to the people with whom I was serving.

I paid special attention to the story of each Medal of Honor recipient as the DIs recounted them as we moved through the Crucible. It felt profound—sacred and monumental, almost. I wanted to understand what made a great Marine. That was also the reason why, when it started raining just three hours into my Crucible and my feet quickly blistered beyond recognition, I decided to hike the ten miles back to the barracks anyway. Because my feet were bleeding so badly, I was offered a ride in the medical van at the end of the second day, but I refused to take it. "Why are you hiking on your tiptoes, Recruit?" the DIs yelled at me, but I was not going to take the easy way out. I was going to stay with my platoon, no matter how much pain I was in.

You end the final hike as the sun is coming up at the parade deck in front of the Iwo Jima memorial. It is there that you are handed your Eagle, Globe, and Anchor insignia, or "EGA" as it is affectionately called. They place the EGA in your left hand and shake your right. At that moment you have officially earned the title Marine. It is a surreal and deeply humbling moment when you are handed that little emblem, because you know you are now a part of an institution, a tradition, and a legacy that stretches back to the birth of our country. You are still in awe of it all the next day when you change out of cammies for the first time and put on your charlies (khaki shirt and green trousers) for Parents' Day, when families are invited to come visit ahead of graduation.

Of course my family was there with all of the Marine T-shirts, signs, noise, and enthusiasm that they bring, and I was thrilled to see them. And it wasn't just my parents or my brothers who came: My grandparents, aunts, uncles, and cousins all descended upon Parris Island to celebrate with me.

On Family Day, the day before graduation, my family had a huge picnic. It was the best meal I'd had in thirteen weeks. The graduation ceremony itself, the following morning, was a bit of a disappointment because instead of passing in formation on the large, iconic parade deck outside, we had to move indoors due to a passing storm; lightning and metal bleachers aren't a great combination.

It was a relief to know boot camp was over. But I broke into a cold sweat when DI Billingsley pulled me aside and asked to talk to me alone for a minute behind the racks in the squad bay.

"Carpenter," he said, "where is your EGA?"

I retrieved my EGA from my cover (military hat) and brought it to him. He took off his drill instructor hat and unscrewed his own insignia, and said, "Here, I want you to have this." He said he saw something special in me, and that he respected my determination to complete the ten-mile hike even though I would have been medically excused from doing so. That was one of the most surprising and impactful moments of my thirteen weeks in boot camp.

Three days later, I had a surprise for Billingsley. I sent him a message via Facebook, thanking him for everything. I was still scared to death of the guy, and some part of me probably will be for the rest of my life, but I also wanted to let him know that his leadership on both the platoon level as well as the personal level had deeply impacted me. He included a little advice in his response: "Take everything we taught you and build on it, keep your nose clean and stay out of trouble and I'll know we did our job."

And he accepted my friend request.

JUNE 2009

We were granted leave after boot camp, and I spent mine back in Lexington. My first morning at home, I woke up around six, shocked to remember what it felt like to wake up on my own instead of having someone bust through the door, flip on the lights, and start screaming. It was strange. I found myself lying there and staring at the ceiling wondering if I was really a Marine or if I just woke up from the most lucid of dreams. I enjoyed a few days of R&R at home before it was back to the Marine world to report to my next duty station—infantry training.

The School of Infantry (SOI) was less than five hours from my house, so my mom offered to drive me there. We sat in silence for much of the drive, unusual for us; usually, Carpenter family road trips involve *a lot* of talking. This trip was scarier in many ways than boot camp because this time I wasn't just a recruit. I now was a Marine, reporting for duty . . . and duty was a school that was going to teach me how to survive in what would likely be the harshest conditions I would ever encounter.

As we rolled through the front gate of the base, I was asked to show my military ID, and I had to identify who was in the car with me so she could be verified, too. As I said, "PFC Carpenter, reporting for SOI. This is my mom," I suddenly realized what it must look like to have my mom dropping me off at SOI as if it were the first day of kindergarten. My mom must have realized it, too, because she suddenly looked horrified and totally embarrassed for me! But thankfully (shockingly), no one seemed to notice or gave me a hard time about it. Looking back, I wouldn't change a thing about that moment.

A number of guys I was with in boot camp joined me at SOI: Griffin Welch, Scott Condrey, Jared Lilly, and Mike Tinari. They used to tease me that I had never done anything *not* by the book in my life—never gotten in trouble and never even eaten a fast food hamburger. That was a bit of a stretch, but probably not that far off. When they met my mom and heard about my dad, though, they laughed and said it all made sense now.

If you were to rank military training centers in terms of how plush they are, Camp Geiger at Marine Corps Air Station New River in North Carolina likely would be close to the bottom. The School of Infantry is a rigorous, two-month-long training designed to teach new Marines the ins and outs of surviving in a combat environment, so it stands to reason that it's not going to be particularly comfortable. The base looks like a Cold War time capsule, with concrete and cinder-block structures and chain-link fences running everywhere.

For the next two months, life consisted of learning how to master various weapons systems that would be so vital to our service in Afghanistan. That, and taking progressively longer hikes where we would dig fighting holes and learn to operate the radio while out in the middle of nowhere. In combat, survival often depends on finding the right balance between caution and action. I think most of us, myself included, are wired for caution. But I knew that in order to be the kind of leader I wanted to be—one who would protect my guys and do what I could to ensure the success of the mission—I had to respond automatically when my brain detected danger. That became one of my main goals at SOI because we all knew that a deployment was coming, wherever we got assigned after graduation. That's what Infantry does: We fight.

When our assignments came down, I couldn't help but feel like we had lucked out. The four of us who roomed together—Griffin, Scott, Mike, and I—had all been assigned to Fox Company, 2nd Battalion 9th Marines, aka "Hell in a Helmet." It had a nice ring to it. In fact, 2/9 is a unit that is only activated in times of combat. They saw some of the most intense action in Vietnam before being disbanded, then were brought back in 2009 to help close down operations in Iraq and to assist future operations in Afghanistan. Today, at the headquarters building for 2/9, the unit colors (our flag) is housed in a glass case with a battle ax next to it and a sign that says, IN CASE OF WAR, BREAK GLASS.

I couldn't have been more excited. However, this enthusiasm quickly turned into fear when the Marines from Fox Company arrived to pick us up and take us to our new unit. Twenty minutes after SOI graduation, the guys assigned to 2/9 were loaded on a bus for the ten-mile drive up the road to Camp Lejeune.

I will never forget the first Marine I saw when we arrived. He had more tattoos than anyone I had ever met before. I distinctly remember that his right arm was covered with a skeleton wearing a top hat and holding a double-barrel shotgun that seemed to point right at anyone looking at it. Yup, that was me: staring down the end of that barrel for the next four years of my life.

I opened the door to my new barracks and experienced one of the most intimidating moments of my Marine Corps career.

The entire platoon of Marines, our new family, had lined the halls in preparation for the new guys. They had just gotten back from a deployment to Iraq and seemed like hungry, caged dogs waiting to be fed. It felt like we were their next meal.

Now, I don't want anyone to get the wrong idea when I say that they hazed us. It wasn't anything dangerous or damaging, though it usually happened in the barracks after the higher-ranking guys went home for the evening. It was mostly typical Marine stuff: a lot of screaming, a lot of "knowledge" classes (from every weapon fact you could imagine, to Marine Corps history, to applying tourniquets, to how to operate radios in a combat environment—you'd be scrubbing the toilets if you didn't know that knowledge), a lot of push-ups and wall-sits (where you balance with your back pressed against the wall with your legs bent at a ninety-degree angle). But if you couldn't handle any of that, then you probably shouldn't ever deploy, because the stress and pressure even in a noncombat deployment environment was a thousand times more intense. Best to get used to it.

2/9 was slated to ship out for a three-month "float" in the fall, sailing to Cuba, Belize, and the Dominican Republic aboard the USS Wasp. Some of the guys would be doing ground exercises and training at Guantanamo Bay Naval Base (GTMO), on the island of Cuba, and the rest would be supporting the Drug Enforcement Agency and Coast Guard with intercepting smugglers.

In preparation for that float, we had a weekend "96" (meaning ninety-six hours of liberty), but we "boots" (Marines who have never deployed) couldn't enjoy it because we had to take a course on helicopter evacuations. It was simultaneously one of the most terrifying and interesting experiences of my life. The helo-dunker, which is essentially a fuselage mounted on a gyroscope, would drop us into a swimming pool as we spun around. A two-minute oxygen canister was our only lifeline as we practiced getting out of our gear. Two minutes might sound like a generous amount of time until you realize the sheer amount of gear you have to shed (rifle, flak jacket, helmet) and how rapidly you breathe when you are panicked. You usually end up burning through all of your oxygen in about thirty seconds. Oh, yeah—and you are *upside down, buckled into your seat, at the bottom of a dark pool, and wearing blackout goggles.* As crazy as that training was, it was also a rush to feel like we were truly preparing for live missions. None of this was theoretical anymore.

By the time we left for our float in September on the USS *Wasp,* we were working toward a deployment-ready bond, especially us younger guys who were trying to earn the respect of our superiors and learning our place with the older guys. I think everyone was anxious to find out when we would head to Afghanistan.

All of us boots drew the undesirable roles on the ship. Some were assigned to cleaning and some to laundry. I had mess duty on the ship. You know what job is even harder than working at a chicken plant? Being a dishwasher on a Navy ship. Breakfast usually runs from six till eight, but the mess staff has to be there an hour and a half to two hours earlier to get everything ready. The kitchen is not air conditioned, and when you're in there with a pile of steaming pots and pans all day, it gets almost unbearable.

The one positive was that I ended up being part of a detachment that actually got to go ashore at GTMO to spend several weeks participating in training exercises, which later proved to be invaluable preparation for Afghanistan. Working in the tropical climate helped reinforce to me the importance of staying hydrated even while pushing through miserable conditions. I'm pretty sure that the higher-ups knew that the deployment surge was coming down the pipeline, and this exercise was part of a pre-deployment workup to help us get used to training all day in the sun at altitude.

We were still on the ship when we got word at the beginning of December that President Obama had confirmed that thirty thousand new troops were going to be sent to Afghanistan. The vast swath of poppy farms in Helmand Province help make Afghanistan the world's largest opium producer, the source for 75–90 percent of the world's illicit opioids (including heroin), according to a U.N. report. One of the main goals of

President Obama's surge in 2010 was to retake Marjah, a key poppy-growing community in Helmand, in order to cut off the flow of drugs and money that was the Taliban's lifeblood for funding weapons, fighters, and bribes.

Cruising through the Caribbean Ocean, we huddled around a small TV that was barely hanging on to a faint signal. Through the static, our Commander in Chief relayed information that was going to change many of our lives forever. "We must deny al-Qaida a safe haven," he said in a televised speech at West Point. "We must reverse the Taliban's momentum and deny it the ability to overthrow the government. And we must strengthen the capacity of Afghanistan's security forces and government, so that they can take lead responsibility for Afghanistan's future." This was it—the announcement we had been waiting for. As soon as we heard news of the surge, we knew we were going to be part of it. My parents had held on to hope up to that point, thinking I might not get deployed, since the U.S. presence in Iraq was winding down. But once the announcement came out, they accepted that this was happening. Personally, I was excited, as were most of the Marines I knew. This was the reason we had joined up, after all—to be part of a mission bigger than ourselves.

I had found what I was looking for in the Marine Corps—mission and meaning. We had a clear objective: to flush the Taliban out of their Helmand Province stronghold in southern Afghanistan, where they were growing never-ending fields of poppies. The poppies became heroin, which was sold to fund weapons and the training of extremists for future terrorist acts, both domestically and around the world. The heroin and other illegal opioids found their way to America, where an opioid epidemic was ravaging the country and claiming tens of thousands of lives each year.

The *Wasp* arrived back in port just before Christmas, and it was special to get to enjoy the holidays at home after three months at sea. But now that I knew I had a deployment on the horizon, I was eager to get back to 2/9 and start preparing.

Regardless of what inevitable dangers lay ahead, I was excited to earn my place in the platoon. That motivation and drive was quickly overshadowed, though, when I was assigned to my four-member fire team. My fire team leader was a disappointment, to be charitable. Everything I had seen, experienced, and been taught about effective leadership was suddenly being contradicted. He yelled without purpose, gave little to no useful instruction, and was one of the slowest guys in physical training every day. How could we trust someone like that to lead us as a four-man infantry team in combat? He didn't seem to care about anything but his next cigarette and getting out of the military. The days, weeks, and months dragged on under his command.

I knew, though, that at the end of the day a poor leader didn't have to affect my individual performance and preparation, and that the rest of our fire team could train to become better Marines with or without his leadership. So, we junior Marines continued to work among ourselves. I almost looked forward to getting my chance to stand up to my team leader, but luckily, it didn't come to that. His behavior caught up to him; he got in trouble and was forced out of the Marine Corps. We caught a break.

The Marine who would fill our old fire team leader's boots would be his opposite in every way. Taryn Heintz was an Eagle Scout, an exceptional person, an exceptional Marine, an exceptional leader—and my saving grace. He was exactly what I had been searching for, opening the door to the barracks. Lance Corporal Heintz seemed more like a teacher than a boss, leading us with patience, understanding, and calmness.

Heintz's style can be summarized in one sentence: Lead with action. Any orders or tasks that Heintz gave us, he had either already done himself or he was absolutely willing to do alongside us. He made sure we ate first; he was the one to work holidays and take the less desirable posts so that his junior guys were taken care of. In short, he earned respect, he didn't demand it. I wanted to follow him until my last breath.

His arrival changed the morale of our entire fire team: The bond of trust and commitment we felt toward one another became unbreakable. I knew that our team would likely be rearranged when we reached Afghanistan, but for now, I had someone modeling exactly the kind of direction and dedication I believed the Marine Corps represented.

As hard as my first experience was, I am thankful to have been exposed to poor leadership so early on. It not only taught me what leadership is not supposed to be like, but also showed me that no matter what is going on around you, or who is in charge, you can still be your own leader and a leader to those around you. I think that experience helped bring the rest of our fire team together. We were going to need it in the months ahead.

Even from our first day as new recruits on Parris Island, we were simultaneously being trained to be leaders and also respectful of orders. It might sound illogical, but it is actually a brilliant way to shape the character and outlook of the next generation of Marines. What I witnessed in that first year of service modeled for me the important balance of confidence and humility, initiative and patience, action and caution. The best leaders aren't the ones who detach themselves from their people or use their authority to avoid responsibility. The leaders who have the most influence and ultimately earn the loyalty of their team are the ones who invest themselves in their people and who willingly shoulder the responsibility that comes with being in charge. I learned from watching the Marines more senior to me—and from being entrusted with a bit of authority myself at boot camp—that being a part of whatever needs to be done, no matter how seemingly menial or unpleasant, goes a long way toward strengthening the bonds of a group. When you know the person in front of you during drills is also willing to be in front of you in a firefight or next to you scrubbing the squad bay, you begin to view the entire mission, and your role in it, differently. A great leader communicates through his or her actions that you are worth their time, effort, energy, and sacrifice. That's when your people will trust you to lead them anywhere—even into the heart of the fight.

And that's exactly where we were headed.

Chapter 6
Someone Else's Shoes

One of the biggest challenges once you know you'll be deploying is the waiting and wondering about what is to come. Your adrenaline levels are elevated. You mentally go over your packing list and double-check your gear about a thousand times. You have your last pizza . . . and then you have another. You say your goodbyes.

Then your ship-out date gets moved.

Or the date gets bumped up and suddenly you are scrambling to squeeze everything in. More often, though, it gets moved back and so you are stuck in the cycle all over again. Even if you aren't excited to go, you get to the point where you just want it to happen because the holding pattern is worse. The anticipation of leaving is the only thing on your mind.

Our leave date bounced around a bit as we moved into the summer of 2010. We heard it might be early July, then that it could be as late as August. While we waited, everyone prepared as best they could. We had a pre-deployment seminar to help inform our family members on how to best support us and prepare them in case their loved one was killed in action. "Family" mostly meant wives and girl-friends; my mom was one of just a handful of mothers there. The seminar was supposed to be comforting in that it gave them a clearer sense of expecta-tions and understanding of protocol, which was, essentially:

If a Marine is killed, next of kin is notified before any further information is released. If you hear about something on the news, don't panic because you would have already been contacted if it was your family member.

Don't be afraid of answering your phone, check-ing your email, or opening your mailbox. Family members are only informed of a death in person, at home, by uniformed officers.

The Marine Corps has crisis counselors and support systems in place to step in immediately should the unimaginable happen.

I'm not sure exactly how comforting that sort of information really was, but I imagine a lot of people still had images in their minds of wives and mothers during World War II receiving news of a death via telegram. I think it helped calm nerves, at least a little, to know that things aren't handled that way anymore. They talked about what would happen when we came home safe and sound, and what would happen if we didn't come home at all. At the time, though, we didn't think about the fact that there was, of course, a third possibility: that we would be wounded. I guess in thinking about the best- and worst-case scenarios, everyone overlooked the middle.

That seminar was eye-opening for me. When members of the military get ready to deploy, nearly all of the attention is directed at the service members who are leaving, but people usually don't realize that we are fine; we have been training to do exactly this for months or years. Our families, however, have not. As I looked around—at the wives juggling three kids, at the women with the pregnant bellies, at the parents struggling to absorb and understand everything they could about this foreign world—I was struck by just how alone we were leaving them all. There were people who were about to be single parents for seven months. There were women who were going to be giving birth or having miscarriages without their partner around. There were children who wouldn't understand why their dad or mom was suddenly gone. Parents and siblings and grandparents who would be isolated and alone. Yes, we were going to a dangerous part of the world, but we had a mission and we had a built-in support structure within our unit. We had countless people praying for us. We had chaplains available for guidance and counseling. We had plenty to keep us busy and care packages from family, friends, and even total strangers to look forward to. We had entire job fields dedicated solely to providing us with whatever we needed.

Our families, on the other hand, had none of that.

I had never really given much thought to the sacrifices of military families up to that day, and the seminar was my first real introduction to the incredible role that they play—a role my family would come to know very well in just a few months.

JULY 2010

Finally, we got an official date. Most of us were excited, as crazy as that sounds. I'm sure there were some guys who really were eager to get to the fight, but for the rest of us, the excitement had more to do with the waiting being over.

We had a few days of pre-deployment leave, so I went home to South Carolina, then my family came to Camp Lejeune to see me off. It's an eerie feeling to give your loved ones a hug and wonder if it is the last one you'll share. For us new guys, anyway, this was the biggest thing we had ever done. Every other adventure up to that point in our lives had come with very few risks. Mission trips, road trips, semesters abroad—sure, there'd always been the risk that something could go wrong, but that would have been unexpected, the exception. On those journeys, the odds had been firmly on our side that everything would go well. Now, we were leaving on a trip where, statistically, it was a given that some of us would never return. As we climbed onto the buses to catch the first leg of our flight, that was a fact we were suddenly unable to ignore. I couldn't help but look around and wonder who wasn't going to be sitting with us on the way home.

As the buses pulled out, we waved goodbye to our families. I looked back at my mom. I had never seen this look on her face before, one of pure desperation. Then they were out of sight.

Highway 17, which runs between Camp Lejeune and Marine Corps Air Station Cherry Point, is a flat highway along a coastal plain, lined with loblollies; there isn't a whole lot to see. It felt like my youth had just been bookended: Your mom and dad wait with you for the bus on your first day of kindergarten and tear up about how fast you're growing as you climb on and ride off. That marks the end of your babyhood, in a way. This experience wasn't all that different, except our packs carried more than crayons and we weren't going to be headed home at the end of the day.

We reached Cherry Point and drove out to the flight line, where I was surprised to see a Ryanair—a commercial airliner from Ireland—plane waiting to take us to Germany. We filed on board and sat in our seats while the flight attendants prepared the cabin for takeoff. We got earbuds to plug into the arm of the seat for the in-flight radio; they even served us meals, just like on a regular flight, which were likely to be our last hot meals for months. Unfortunately I slept through mine, although I didn't sleep as much as I should have on that flight because my buddy Scott Condrey and I took turns waking one another up every time "Alejandro" by Lady Gaga came on over the headsets. The song had just been released and, in a way, represented to us all the basic, pop-culture stuff we were going to be isolated from for the next seven months. I didn't even really like the song but listening to it felt like one last grasp to hold on to the fluff that doesn't matter, yet makes you feel connected to the outside world.

The flight was so weirdly normal that it would have been easy to forget I wasn't going on vacation . . . except for the fact that I was wearing cammies and holding a machine gun between my knees. In fact, all of our military-issued weapons and gear were either loaded in the luggage compartment or stowed in the overhead bins. I kept thinking that I was living in a Venn diagram, and the circle representing the "normal," civilian life and the circle representing the military world were intersecting in a surreal way.

We had a short layover in Germany—only a few hours—then we pushed on to Kuwait. From Kuwait we flew to Kyrgyzstan, where, though it was the end of July and close to one hundred degrees in the valley where the U.S. base is, we could look up and see snow-covered mountains surrounding us. Everything was a little dreamlike, but at the same time, I knew that reality was about to hit us in the face. With each leg we were inching closer to what was then the worst combat zone on earth: Helmand Province in southern Afghanistan.

Still, it was impossible to comprehend exactly what we were about to encounter. We were all excited and amped to get over there, but I think for most of us, we were really just coming from a place of having played combat video games or watched war movies. Even the guys who had deployed before to Iraq had been there as tensions started to calm down; none of us was prepared for the reality of Afghanistan. I guarantee that if you were to ask anyone who said he was excited on the trip out how he felt on the trip home, he would probably just kind of chuckle and say, "What was I thinking? How stupid. Why was I excited for what we went through?"

It's hard not to feel invincible. First, the Marine Corps trains you so well that you know you are part of one of the most elite fighting forces on earth; it seems impossible that the forty-year-old Soviet weapons and homemade detonating devices of the Taliban could possibly pose a serious risk. Second, you're in your late teens or early twenties, and the risk-reward center of the brain is not fully developed, so the possibility of danger seems thrilling rather than sobering. It's hard to think about death when the world seems so full of life, possibility, and excitement. You feel invincible because, up to this point, you basically have been. Broken arm from falling out of a tree fort? No problem; the doctors can fix you right up by putting you in a cast for a month. Concussion from a bad hit in football? Concerning, but you'll probably bounce back in a few weeks. When that is your frame of reference, it's hard to imagine the degree of injury that might be awaiting you. If you *can* imagine it, it still seems like something that would happen to someone else.

The problem is that you are everyone else's "someone else."

I had no idea, as I gazed down at the desolate landscape from the helicopter that was inserting us into Marjah, that so many shades of brown and green could exist. As the fields under us passed by, I began to wonder: *Am I going to die in one of these fields?* My gaze was interrupted by one of the helicopter crew members stepping in front of me and casually handing me a belt of ammunition for my M249 SAW as he screamed over the noise of the engines, "We're going to be taking contact when we land." I had no idea how laughable the idea of invincibility is in the face of war.

HELMAND PROVINCE, AFGHANISTAN
Autumn 2010

There is a scene in *Forrest Gump* where Forrest and Bubba join up with their unit in Vietnam, only to find that there are steaks grilling and music playing, and nothing looks at all like they expected an active war zone to look. That wasn't quite my experience, but I was definitely blown away by the creativity of

Marines to make even the most grim, austere conditions more livable and even enjoyable. We didn't have many luxuries, but someone had received a volleyball in a care package and a couple of guys had immediately set to work weaving a net out of 550 cord so that they could set up a decent court on the hard-packed dirt ground of our compound. It was a great morale booster in between patrols until we started hearing *ratta-tat-tat-tat-tat* from outside the perimeter every time the ball volleyed to the other side. It was gunfire from local Taliban, who didn't want to get close enough to do real damage, so instead settled for trying to pop our ball.

The area around Marjah is incredibly flat, and we could see the nearest village, about one thousand yards from our compound. Every time the ball rose above the walls, the shooter there would fire frantically. The bullets would fly right over the compound, so no one was ever in danger of being hit by them, but the situation struck us as strangely hilarious—as if a popped volleyball would devastate us and send all the Americans packing. And even if our Taliban killjoy had managed to succeed in hitting the ball, we had others. A couple guys had written home about our "court," and people kept sending us balls: volleyballs, footballs, even a basketball, though we were never able to rig up a hoop because it wasn't worth the risk of being exposed over the walls long enough to do so, and the rocky dirt floor of our compound wasn't the best surface anyway.

Despite the levity, there were times when the reality of a combat zone shone through. We didn't jump into patrols on day one; there was a kind of leadership-training down period. The higher-ranking Marines went out on patrol first to get a feel for things before leading patrols of their own. It was a way to help everyone get acclimated to being outside the wire. But our time to step into an active role came quickly enough.

My first patrol took place four or five days after we arrived. We stopped at a compound at the end of a road, after pausing to talk to the owner about his family, the area, and whether he had seen any Taliban nearby. As expected, he had, so while the other guys started to fan out, I set up my SAW across the street from the man's house, next to a low, mud-brick shed; just like hundreds of others in the region, it was used for drying out the marijuana and poppy crops that help fund the Taliban.

As I lay on my stomach behind my gun, scanning the landscape, I remember thinking that the field before me was a perfect rectangle, as if it had been laid out with a ruler. In a region where so much is scattershot, adapted to the land, it was unusual to see something so precise. It was oddly beautiful.

All of a sudden, it was as if the skies had opened and the clouds were dumping hail: So many rounds were hitting the ground around me that I couldn't even see through my scope for all the dust they were kicking up. There was a *thunk* as a bullet ricocheted off the side of the shed, and at almost exactly the same time, I felt something hit my lower back, about two inches to the right of my spine, just above my belt line and below my body armor—probably the only inch of skin that wasn't protected.

"I'm hit!" I yelled, grabbing my gun and leaping about ten feet behind me to where my buddies were holding security. Two thoughts raced through my brain: Did bullet wounds really not hurt as much as I had imagined, or did I just have so much adrenaline in my system that I wasn't registering the pain? And after an hour outside the wire, was I already a casualty? I was furious that I wouldn't get to contribute anything to the effort if this stupid Taliban bullet sent me home. I couldn't imagine leaving my guys behind because of an injury on our very first patrol.

As I bounced back, another Marine instantaneously moved forward to man the end-of-the-road security position while the corpsman checked me out behind the compound. Amazingly, the bullet had not penetrated the skin, but it did leave a dark bruise, almost like a paintball fired at point-blank range. I was hurting, but grateful my tour wasn't over quite so quickly. The mark grew uglier for well over a week as the blood pooled, then finally started to fade; and since there was no real damage done, I conveniently left out any mention of it in my letters home. In fact, I didn't tell my mom until at least three or four years afterward.

Not every patrol was that exciting, but we always had to be prepared. We traveled in squads of around twelve and fire teams of four men, plus our medic. The guy carrying the radio is often the first person the enemy tries to take out so that you can't immediately call for backup, but the Taliban also loves to go for the corpsmen. Losing them would leave the entire squad vulnerable in an entirely different and far more urgent way, so we always made sure they had a little extra protection.

"Hey, Doc," I would say before we went out. "Let me go first, because if I get blown up, you can take care of me. But if you get blown up, I don't know how to save you."

The corpsman would laugh and say, "Sure, Carpenter. Steal all the fun." But corpsmen usually agreed to let other Marines go in front, not because they were afraid but because they understood the importance of their role. Sometimes, though, there was no way of anticipating from where an attack would come.

One day in late September or early October, our lieutenant ordered my squad to conduct a vehicle control point (VCP) at an intersection along an empty stretch of road next to a village. We stayed out there for several hours as we gathered census data on the local population. Around one in the afternoon, we were wrapping up one of the few stop-and-searches of the day as the sun baked us alive. We wondered what the point was of this effort since we hadn't seen many people and certainly hadn't apprehended any bad guys.

Nick Eufrazio, my best friend, was out of the canal and exposed when all of a sudden, bullets started to hail down on us. While we had been manning the VCP, Taliban had set up three shooters no more than a hundred yards away, at different angles, in what's called a "bear paw" formation, to try to triangulate and wipe us out. We could see their heads as they ran along the canals by the tree line. I happened to be positioned by the compound on the other side of the road. Lance Corporal Stringer, the team leader at the time, peered over the edge of the canal to see if our guys could safely return fire, when his head flew backward like he had been punched. It looked like a bullet had gone straight into his forehead. For a moment he sat perfectly still, blinking in a daze, then he shook it off. Miraculously, the bullet had struck his helmet and the Kevlar had done its job, warping the track of the bullet so that it skimmed the edge of his helmet rather than lodging in his skull.

I had a two-hundred-round drum already loaded onto my Squad Automatic Weapon, so I called to the guys, "Get ready to move when I turn the corner of this building." I prepared to unload. I turned the corner of the compound, pressed my finger on the trigger, and didn't let up while the other guys ran in a crouched position down the dried-up canal before hopping out to cross the road and take cover in the compound until the firefight was over. Doc Frend told me later that he could see the bullets striking the wall right next to my head and body as at least one of the shooters turned his weapon on me. Nick, who had been lobbing grenades in the direction of the shooters in an effort to clear the area long enough to give the other guys a chance to run, was the last of our guys to cross. At exactly the moment he made it across the road and behind the wall, I ran out of rounds. For the next two hours we were engaged in an intense firefight until mortarman Corporal Vance Rath was able to respond to our radio calls back at base, and dropped mortars on the Taliban with pinpoint precision from almost two miles out. After we were confident that there were no active shooters left, we approached the shooters' position to do a battlefield damage assessment (BDA). Bullet casings littered the ground. Those guys had been busy.

Incredibly, none of our men were injured that day, but the incident shook us up; our squads had already taken an incredible beating that autumn. What had initially started as a platoon of three fire squads broke up into four in order to cover more ground, but we lost so many guys we had to reorganize and combine back down to three.

No matter how mentally prepared you think you are, you will never be ready for that first fight, let alone that first casualty. A guy gets blown apart by an IED or takes a bullet to the chest, and suddenly, everything you've ever believed about the world collapses in a moment. I turned twenty-one on October 17, but the day really didn't make me feel any older; my experiences in Afghanistan, however, felt like they aged me years at a time.

In fact, my birthday was as surreal as everything else. One of my best friends, Griffin, gave me a birthday card made out of notebook paper and promised to take me out for a beer when we got home; he had done the same thing for Jared Lilly's twenty-first the month before. Never mind that Griffin was barely eighteen so he wouldn't be able to drink for another three years—he was someone who could charm a waitress into letting him buy a round for the table even without a valid ID. I imagined we'd all go to Texas Roadhouse, since we ate there at least once a week back in North Carolina anyway, and we'd toast to a successful deployment and to turning twenty-one in the middle of nowhere in southern Afghanistan. But first, I had to make it through the next patrol.

We had left early in the afternoon on my birthday, and were now trying to make it back to Patrol Base Beatley by nightfall. It had been a four-hour game of cat and mouse. As we had entered one patch of woods, our patrol had frozen midstep as the dreaded sound of M203 fire echoed around us. A 203 is a grenade launcher that attaches to the bottom of a rifle and when fired makes a distinct *thump* sound, followed by an anxious wait to see where that deadly *thump* impacts. Immediately, our squad leader got on the radio to tell the other half of our squad to stop firing 203s until we could get their exact location. We had intentionally split up to cover more ground, but during the intense fighting through thick tree lines and scattered villages, we had become unsure of our exact proximity to one another.

A voice crackled back over the radio, "That's not us. Those are not our 203s." In an instant, we went from frozen to executing some quick maneuvers to find cover. For the first time in three months, the enemy was launching grenades at us. Happy birthday to me.

As we were running through the woods of Afghanistan, praying that our enemy had terrible aim, I had a weird flashback to the last time I was in this position: playing paintball in the woods as a kid, with my only care being to grab the other team's flag. The consequences of losing *that* gunfight were a bruise and a loss of bragging rights.

Maneuvering out of the tree line, we approached a compound on the outskirts of the village we were nearing. As usual, family livestock were hanging out around the home. Two goats were tied up to a tree, and chickens strutted around pecking at the ground. We slowed down, just in time to hear another dreaded *thump* from the 203. The scene couldn't have been scripted more perfectly: The grenade ripped through the air and struck a chicken, vaporizing it in an instant. I felt terrible for the chicken, but part of me had to laugh because I was just relieved that our latest casualty wasn't another Marine.

Before the battle was over I vividly remember crawling through a field with my weapon on my back, holding the barrel over my shoulder to keep it as clean as possible. Crawling just under the trajectory of the incoming bullets, I couldn't help but think how strange it was that I might not even make it to enjoy my first legal beer.

We eventually made it back to PB Beatley safely, but I couldn't shake the image of that unfortunate chicken. It was there one instant, and then it was simply . . . gone. Little did I know that, just a few weeks later, I would be able to empathize with that bird.

We had heard about how dangerous Helmand Province was, and we knew on an intellectual level that it was going to be a rough deployment. Even so, there really is no way to prepare yourself to get shot at every day, battling for your life in a firefight, having to constantly scan the ground so you don't step on an explosive but seeing it happen anyway, watching your buddies and your leaders bleed out. If I had been on a combat deployment before, I would have had a different perspective going in—less excitement and more resignation. There really isn't any way to predict how someone will respond to that kind of stress, until they live through it. Your brain doesn't have a category for a real-life scenario of "Now I am being shot at, so I will react in this way." No matter how much you turn it over in your head, it's all still hypothetical until you are in the thick of it. Even then, your reaction might be different from one situation to another, based on how much trauma you've already experienced. And there is no way to predict what the effect of that trauma will be on the guy next to you, either.

You can't dwell on it too long, though, or you could drive yourself crazy. Everyone had their own ways of coping with the stress; the key was to stay busy and distract yourself. When we weren't putting our poor volleyball at risk, we were sitting around the table enjoying the spoils of care packages: books, magazines, music, and card games. Heintz loved showering—not that it was a legit shower; you just poured water over your head from a bag or carton that was rigged up, and it would evaporate off you before you could actually wash—but those "showers" seemed to be his way of wiping away the awful stuff of the day. Some guys wrote letters, other napped. There were always a few guys who would work out obsessively, even though someone would inevitably make some crack about how they were trying to look good for their coffin. That kind of gallows humor keeps you from losing your mind.

We still had to stand post every day, so that occupied our time, too. The guys I really felt bad for were our corpsmen, because they never had a chance to completely decompress; locals would come to the gate and ask for medical care and our guys would always oblige them. Always. What might seem like a pretty minor injury to us at home could become life-threatening for the Afghan people, given a remote setting lacking sanitation and follow-up care. Our medics would occasionally run little clinics for locals who were sick. We got to know a lot of familiar faces from Marjah. Men would walk up—only men ever came—sometimes with their hands in the air, and the Marine on post would tell them to stop. The interpreter (or "terps," as they were nicknamed) would approach the man and ask what he needed. If he wanted to see a doctor, he would get patted down. Then he'd either be blindfolded as he was taken to the medical facility so he could not see what we had in our compound, or else one of our docs would just treat him at the back door. They would put in some sutures and maybe give him a pain reliever or antibiotic so the injury wouldn't get infected, and then tell the patient to come back in a week so they could take out the sutures.

Kids would arrive who had been hurt by farming tools or who had taken a bad fall or who had burns on their hands from picking up spent bullet casings when they were still hot. One child had fallen into the open cooking fire that every Afghan home has, and burned his face. Sometimes the docs would even see children who had been shot accidentally. It was actually helpful for us when they treated the children, because kids tend to be chatty, and we often learned where IED trip wires had been laid just from listening to the kids talk about where they were playing when they got hurt. Eventually, we started noticing a horrible pattern: A child would come in with an injury, spill the beans about where an explosive had been planted, we would go and detonate it, and a day or two later the same child would show up with lacerations or bruises. You could put two and two together.

The same adults who were trying to kill us were eager for the Americans to treat their children. It felt weird thinking, *Your dad wants to kill me but we hope you don't get tetanus.* But our corpsmen would treat anyone who came to them. Our medics would go patch them up. They couldn't call in a medevac helicopter in the middle of a firefight for a civilian, but the doc would tell any injured, non-Taliban Afghans to drive to our base and then either he would give them a note with instructions for whoever was on duty to call in a medevac, or else we would radio over to let the base know someone was coming who needed help. They would fly the more critical patients over to Camp Leatherneck or Camp Dwyer, where there were better facilities to treat them. The doctors would clean their wounds, stitch them up, and then give them notes about follow-up care to show us when they got back home. It wasn't the kids' or the civilians' fault they were in the wrong place at the wrong time or that they had been engulfed by a war zone. Sometimes, the kids had parents who were fighting for the Taliban but didn't want to; they did so in order to keep their family from being injured or murdered.

The only time I can think of when our medics refused to treat someone was when it was clear that their injury was a trap. For example, there was a guy we spotted laying out an IED. He took off on his motorcycle when he realized he'd been spotted, and we couldn't help but crack up laughing when he wiped out in his hurry to get away. A few hours later, the same guy approached the gate with road rash, asking if we could help him. There was no way to know what his actual intent was—did he really want help from us or was he wearing a suicide vest in the hope of finishing the job he started with the IED? Our docs told him to go to Lashkar Gah, where the nearest hospital was, and sent him away.

Those exchanges between the medical staff and the locals affected me. It amazed me to see how seriously the corpsmen took the Hippocratic oath in how they treated the civilian population, and to see how the civilian population overlooked political differences or risked angering the local warlords when their children needed help. It made me wonder what my life would look like if I'd been born in Afghanistan rather than the United States.

Some of the most vivid memories I have of being deployed are lying down at night, staring up at the stars, and watching passenger planes fly overhead, just tiny blinking specks in the vast, dark Afghanistan sky. Helmand Province cuts straight through the center of the lower half of the country. Afghans who needed to get across the country, if they had any money at all, would fly rather than attempt to cross an active war zone by car or motorcycle. It was bizarre to be there on the ground, lying in the dirt, watching the blinking lights of the planes overhead, thinking about the people up there. They were probably warm and comfortable, and had no idea that an American who hadn't had a shower in months was watching them from the ground, wondering what their life was like. I felt at once totally separate from, and yet somehow very much connected with, those strangers flying above me.

Watching the airplanes made me think a lot about the expression "Someone, somewhere is having the worst day of their life" and how we are so often surrounded by pain, fear, and suffering that is invisible to us. I would lie on the cold ground, seventy-five hundred miles from home, wondering about the people sipping drinks thirty thousand feet above me—and realize that I was the person having the worst day.

That experience of feeling invisible but watching someone else go about their normal business is one of the most powerful lessons I brought home from Afghanistan. Was I *really* seeing people? As I moved from one place to another, just living out my day-to-day life, who was watching me from afar? The corpsmen saw the patients and they saw the need; they didn't see the political divisions or tribal affiliation or social standing of the people in front of them. I think a lot about the Afghan people who were threatened with violence if they didn't raise a gun against the Americans; on the surface it would be easy to classify them all as "the enemy," but some of them just wanted to be left alone to raise their families in peace. How quickly did I dismiss people based on circumstances I didn't fully understand? And what about the way people react to extremely high stress, high stakes situations? Previously, I might have regarded someone's panic or coping mechanisms as a sign of weakness, but that was because I had never lived with this kind of pressure and trauma before. I know now how the horrific casualties I witnessed deeply impacted *me*, but what about the perspective of the guy who got hit? What about his family? In an instant, their lives changed forever in ways I couldn't fathom. I started asking myself, *When I am having an un-showered-dehydrated-meal-far-away-from-my-home kind of day, how do I react? How do I view myself? And what does it mean that there are still people out there—millions of them—who still have it worse than I do?*

They say there are no atheists in foxholes; I think maybe we all become philosophers in combat outposts, as well.

Chapter 7
The Grenade

PATROL BASE DAKOTA: HELMAND PROVINCE, AFGHANISTAN
Sunday, November 21, 2010—approximately 1:00 P.M. (3:30 A.M. Eastern Standard Time)

*I*t is hot and everything is covered in a fine layer of dust—our gear, our uniforms, our skin. It's a relief to be still for the moment rather than having to go out on patrol; then again, when you're walking, somehow the sun doesn't seem to be quite as intense, as if it is baking you on the spot. The compound where we have set up is small and relatively calm. Life seems to be going on just as it normally would, as if half-a-dozen Marines weren't operating out of one of the houses. Normally, a tiny cluster of homes like this would make scanning for suspicious activity pretty easy, but there is only a two-story rooftop that hasn't collapsed, which means we can't get as full a view of the entire compound as we'd like without exposing more of ourselves than is safe. You never know when the enemy could be watching, ready to strike.

Nick and I are on post, sitting against our Afghan "sandbag recliners," joking about getting off the roof if a grenade makes it to us. Presumably, there is a soft sound and a small puff of dust as something lands near our feet, but I don't remember it.

All I know is that my body reacts instinctively before my mind even registers what it is. Then, suddenly, it feels like I've been hit really hard in the face and I can't see a thing—it's as if I am looking at a TV with no connection, just white and gray static. My ears are ringing extremely loudly but my body is numb.

There is no connection, no through line, no logical progression of events; I just remember heat, laughter, and then a massive impact as all of my senses go haywire for reasons I can't explain.

Everything happened at once. Two grenades exploded, but those landed in the courtyard of the compound; the openness of the courtyard and the old mud-and-straw walls, solid as concrete from centuries of baking in the sun, absorbed most of the blast. A third grenade was a dud. A fourth grenade must have been lobbed a bit higher than the others by whoever threw the lot at us, because it landed on the second-story roof where Nick and I were perched.

What happened next I'm not certain. The last thing I remember clearly is laughing with Nick before starting to move toward something. But in the weeks and years after, several investigations—including an extensive review done in advance of the Medal of Honor decision—dug deeply into the events of the next few seconds of my life. While writing this book I requested and read, for the first time, that Medal of Honor investigation. What showed up on those pages felt surreal. Working off that report and conversations with those who saved my life, here's what I know.

According to the official report:

[F]our eyewitnesses . . . saw Lance Corporal Carpenter rise up to a standing or kneeling position immediately prior to the blast; multiple eyewitnesses . . . saw Lance Corporal Carpenter's body lying directly over the blast hole immediately after the grenade detonated. . . . [T]he Explosive Ordnance Disposal staff noncommissioned officer attached to the platoon . . . provided his expert opinion that the grenade had to have been covered by a heavy object to blast through the roof, and that the significant damage to Lance Corporal Carpenter's Personal Protective Equipment, particularly his Small Arms Protective Insert (SAPI) plate carrier, was consistent with the grenade detonating immediately under, or in close proximity to, his body.

In other words, I threw myself over the grenade, apparently. I don't remember thinking about it, and I certainly don't recall actually doing it. I only remember the aftereffects. A few seconds after the strange assault on my senses, I tried to shake it off and push my body up, but I couldn't feel my arms. With every ounce of strength I possessed, I worked to push myself up, but my body simply would not respond. The disorientation was overwhelming: Five seconds before, everything had been normal. Suddenly, I was numb and vaguely aware that I probably should be in pain, but I could feel nothing at all. I knew I was alive so I knew I must be okay, but nothing made sense. Why couldn't I see? What was that deafening roar that was blocking out every other sound? Where was I? And why was everything numb?

Calm down and think. The last thing I remember is being on the roof, I reasoned in my head. *I wonder what could have injured me this badly on a roof—or did I get off the roof and I went on patrol and all of this is just going on in my head? Maybe I stepped on an IED and the last thing I remember is being on that roof.*

As I was puzzling through these questions, all of them racing through my mind in a split second, my confusion grew even deeper as I realized that someone was pouring warm water all over me. *What was happening?* Nothing made sense and I had no context to even try to make sense out of it. I was on the roof, talking to Nick, then . . . this. Whatever *this* was. As I searched for answers, my brain was furiously putting pieces together to create some kind of meaning. And then it clicked: This wasn't water—it was blood. I was bleeding out.

At that same moment, I tried to call for help, but the only thing I could feel was my tongue searching for my lower jaw—no cheeks, no teeth, no jaw. It was as if the bottom part of my mouth had disappeared. A seed of panic started to grow inside me: *Was I just in shock, or was I really missing part of my face?*

According to the reports, a great friend and one of the greatest Marines I have ever known, Jared Lilly, had been watching us from the stairs and was the first one to the roof just seconds after the explosion. He immediately screamed for Doc Frend. Normally, Doc would have stayed downstairs until we had a chance to sweep the perimeter to make sure that there was no one hiding in an effort to ambush our medic, but Jared knew there was no time for that.

Doc came pounding up the shaky bamboo ladder from the room below and saw me lying facedown on the sandbags. With one glance, he sized up the scene, and realized that even though it was probably too late for me, Nick had a chance. He had taken shrapnel to the forehead that had blown up and under his helmet—not good, but he was still breathing. Well, kind of. The reports said it was more of a snoring sound as his body struggled to pull air into his lungs, so Doc went to work stabilizing him while the rest of our guys radioed for medevacs and backup. Doc put a nasopharyngeal airway in for Nick to help him breathe—basically, a tube down the nose to the back of the throat—and Nick started foaming at the mouth, so Doc ordered him off the roof in order to get him in a more stable place to work on him and also in case anyone opened fire or tossed another grenade. Rather than trying to carry him down the stairs and risk jostling him, a couple of our tallest Marines rushed to the side of the building and Nick was lowered down to them. Meanwhile, Jared and a couple other guys ventured over to me and realized that I was still breathing, too. But any optimism they had that I might be okay evaporated when they rolled over my body, which was still smoking.

Remember that I am not a big guy, so the amount of surface area that was able to absorb the blast was pretty minimal. Not that a human body of any size was designed to deflect grenade explosions, but basic physics tells us that between a larger body and a smaller body covering a grenade, the impact is going to be a bit more concentrated on the smaller body. Given there was a hole in the solid roof from the explosion, and looking at the extent of my injuries, Doc didn't even believe I was still alive until he saw that I was struggling to breathe. He told me later that two thoughts kept running through his head as he got to work on me: *How did he possibly survive the initial blast?* and *How did this not kill someone Carpenter's size?*

My cammies were soaked, as if someone had dumped a bucket of blood on me, and my jaw was severed, sliced in two. The guys said later it was like the monster in *Predator.* My tongue was dangling limply and my mouth was exposed all the way back to my uvula—that thing that hangs down the back of the throat. What was left of my teeth were in a jumble in my mouth and scattered on the ground.

The question, of course, was where to begin. Corpsmen are trained in the basics of battlefield triage—how to treat basic wounds and how to keep people alive in dire conditions until they can be evacuated to a hospital. They are amazing—superhuman, actually—at what they do. But nowhere in his training had Doc encountered any lesson on how to treat survivors after a point-blank grenade explosion, because there usually *aren't* survivors.

Blood was on every inch of my body. My body armor was torn and mangled, and a huge portion of my face was hanging off my skull and onto my shoulder, which clearly had shrapnel embedded in it. Doc could see that I was struggling to breathe, so he started there by putting an airway in before they took me off the roof. He could figure out how to put Humpty Dumpty back together again after they got me on the ground. But he had a choice to make. Normally, with a fractured face, an oral pharyngeal would be the way to go, but I didn't have any jaw left to help create the airway, so he only had three choices. He could cut my throat open with his pocketknife to create an airway—which was even more terrifying than it sounds, because he didn't have a mask or a bag to help me breathe, so he would have had to do the breathing for me through a rubber Camelbak tube from our hiking canteens.

Or he could do a CRIC (cricothyrotomy) through my nose and down the back of my throat to create an artificial airway as I was choking on blood, but he didn't have a CRIC kit, either. Or I could somehow figure out how to breathe on my own. But I was still choking, so he realized he was going to have to improvise with that same pocketknife and Camelbak tube to rig up a CRIC. That wasn't the sort of thing they taught when he was preparing to be a medic, presumably because they never anticipated a fire team would run into so many casualties in such little time to exhaust their supplies.

He put a device into my nose to support the tube, and that sensation was the trigger that jerked me back to consciousness and made me start coughing. Doc needed to lay me down to finish the procedure, but he was afraid of all my teeth fragments falling back into my throat so he kept me sitting upright as he worked. I kept trying to talk, but it only sounded like gurgling water from all the blood and tissue blocking my throat. Even though they couldn't understand a word, my attempt at speaking was a good thing because Doc saw that my body was somehow still functional enough to keep me breathing, and decided not to risk the CRIC after all. As he pulled the plug from my nose, a huge stream of mucus and blood came with it, and I suddenly began to take in air more easily. With my breathing stabilizing a bit, they handed me down to McLaughlin, our waiting tall guy, and he laid me on the ground while Doc and the rest of my buddies ran down the stairs to get back to work and provide cover.

Once we were on the ground, Doc set to working on my arm. He wanted to put a tourniquet on it, but everywhere he grabbed was like a wet noodle. The bones had been splintered into so many pieces that there was absolutely nothing solid enough to anchor it so he could tie it off. Finally, he placed the tourniquet at my armpit, as high as he could possibly go, because that was the only place there was any bone left that was even remotely solid. After that, he did a needle thoracentesis, which would allow any air trapped in my lungs to escape and then permit my lungs to reinflate more fully.

My good friend Scott Condrey showed up with his fire team just a few minutes later; they were out on patrol nearby when they heard the explosions and came running. He told me later he was trying to say goodbye to me, but I couldn't understand a word anyone was saying, even though they were screaming in my ears. My eyes were wide open and I seemed fully conscious, but everything sounded like it was coming through a can on a string a mile away. I kept asking them if I was going to die and apologizing for everything. "Is Nick okay? Is Nick okay? I'm sorry I got hurt," I repeated over and over. "I'm so sorry this happened. Please tell my parents I'm sorry."

"You're not going to die," they kept reassuring me as they prepped me to board the helicopter. "We're here for you. We won't let you die." As they scrambled to wrap me in combat gauze—thin strips of fabric infused with something to help coagulate the blood—they kept assuring me I was going to be fine, even though none of them believed it. Sometimes, lying is the kindest thing you can do.

Amazingly, there were two helicopters already in the area performing medical evacuations for other Marines, so the first one touched down only twelve minutes after Nick and I were injured. Given that it had taken almost fifty minutes for a medevac to reach Zach Stinson nearly two weeks before, this was a miracle. While our team worked frantically inside the compound, other Marines secured the LZ (landing zone) field behind the compound for the medevac bird to land. Doc was still afraid of laying me down and risking blood or teeth falling back into my throat, so my buddies rigged up a makeshift chair stretcher with a poncho liner—a kind of blanket Marines carry with them in the field—and they ran me to the helicopter that way, adjusting their arms as they carried me to keep me in a sitting position. Doc pulled out his last morphine shot to try to ease my pain during transport, but the thin needle tip snagged on the combat gauze on my leg and bent so he couldn't administer the morphine. "I'm so sorry, man," was all he could say as they loaded me on the bird.

All I remember is that I knew I only had seconds left, so I thought about my family and how devastated they were going to be and how it would destroy my mom when I didn't make it home. And then I said a quick prayer for forgiveness for anything I had done wrong. I was trying to make the best and most of my last few seconds here on earth . . . and then everything became suddenly and strangely tranquil. I felt a deep exhaustion—an exhaustion unlike any other, an exhaustion impossible to recount, an exhaustion that completely consumed me—and I felt myself fading away. I was totally at peace with the fact.

I had no way of knowing that things were just getting started for the rest of my buddies. When they came running after hearing the blast, third squad secured the perimeter for two medevacs to come for Nick and me, and then they ascertained where the guy who threw the grenades had come from. They called in more Marines for QRF (Quick Reaction Force) and for gunships, which are airplanes or helicopters heavily armed with machine guns and sometimes cannons, too, to bring the rain to eliminate anyone else who might be planning a second attack. Just minutes after the medevac bird took off, one of the engineers of third squad came around the corner of the compound and stepped on an IED. Lucky for him, he only caught the edge of it so his face was peppered with shrapnel but his legs were okay. Meanwhile, a firefight broke out as local Taliban started firing rockets at our position. One hit right next to the door of the compound, and the barrage kept coming.

My buddies remarked later what a beautiful sound it was to hear the inbound Cobra helicopters as they reached the scene; they flew so low that you could make out the door gunner throwing up devil horns with his hand as he took aim at the tree line with the minigun—a six-barrel machine gun that can fire up to six thousand rounds per minute. Then the Hellfire missiles came in from the Cobras, and at the very end they did a show of force with a jet; it just flew by and made a loud noise, but it sounded absolutely terrifying if you didn't know it was on your side. After about a half hour of relentless attack, the firing stopped.

As Nick and I were being unloaded at the combat hospital at nearby Camp Bastion, Jared was slumped against the wall of the compound staring at his hands, which were still covered in my blood. He had a cigarette in his mouth, but his tears were falling so hard that they kept putting it out. Doc Frend had the blood of five different Marines on his uniform at that point. It had been the worst two hours any of us could have imagined.

Third squad took over securing PB Dakota while my squad was headed back to the main base, PB Beatley. They still had a two-click walk ahead of them, which wasn't that long but felt like a marathon after what they had just experienced. As they looked forward to shedding their gear and decompressing, I was being prepped for surgery.

GILBERT, SOUTH CAROLINA
Sunday, November 21, 2010—12:00 P.M. Eastern Standard Time (7:30 P.M. Afghanistan)

Mom had left her phone in the car during church and came back out after the service to find it full of messages. Jill, Nick's girlfriend, had received word that Nick had been injured and she knew the two of us were usually together. Mom immediately checked to see if she or Dad had missed any calls informing them about me, but nothing showed up, so she assumed I was safe and passed word along with assurances they were praying for Nick and asked for updates. As soon as they got home, Mom went to the computer and accessed her Sunday school's private page, requesting special prayers for Nick. She had a sinking feeling as she realized that Nick and I were always together. "We should make sure we have checked all avenues of communication," she told my dad. "Emails, cellphones, the answering machine . . ."

That was when she noticed the light on our answering machine was blinking. She started to whisper, "No, no, no, no, no, no . . ." as she pressed the button. A man's voice came on, and everyone froze:

This is Gunnery Sergeant Tart with the United States Marine Corps here in Quantico, Virginia. Sir, ma'am . . . if this is James and Robin Carpenter, please give us a call at your earliest convenience or as soon as you hear this message . . . This is in reference to your son, William. Please give us a call at your earliest convenience.

There was a moment of silence, then my dad replayed the message and copied down the phone number before furiously dialing it. He got ahold of Gunny Tart, who told my dad everything they knew at that point, which was still preliminary. Gunny Tart gave my dad a number he could call for updates, which my dad dialed the moment he hung up. No answer. My mom turned and walked out of the kitchen into her and Dad's room. She lay on the bed, facedown, motionless. Price and Peyton just stared at each other, unsure of what to do.

My parents started reaching out to everyone they knew—a radiologist Mom worked with, folks from church—for prayers. Their Sunday school teacher, Scott Vaughan, put a lot of things in motion, connecting them with people he thought might be able to help. Neighbors and friends started pouring in as word spread. It was sheer chaos. All the while, every thirty minutes Dad kept calling the number Gunny Tart provided, but there were never any updates.

They didn't hear anything else for nearly twenty-four hours.

Chapter 8
Call Your Mom

Reconstructing this part of my story is difficult for several reasons, primarily because I remember none of it. The events, as I am describing them, are pieced together from recollections of the people who were with me and from what I can find in my military records. I simply have to accept most of this on faith and acknowledge that there are always going to be several weeks of my life I will never be able to account for. Even though I know very little about this crucial part of my story, it can't be left out. So here we go.

I do know this: There are two types of miracles. The first kind of miracle is when one amazing thing happens, and there is no explaining how or why. The second kind is when there is a massive line of dominoes set up that all have to fall precisely the right way and at the right time for something to work out.

This piece of my life is the second kind of miracle.

It's impossible to follow the string all the way back, but if I were forced to pick a first moment when the chips started falling in my favor, it would have to be when there were already medevac helicopters in the area, and mine arrived within twelve minutes of the explosion. Miracle.

Then there was the morphine needle—the one with which Doc Frend tried to give me an injection but that got snagged on the thin combat gauze. Doc did everything perfectly in terms of my triage care, and his attempt to administer the drug was exactly the right thing to do in that situation. However, due to the nature of my injuries, the doctors told me later that had even the slightest drop of morphine entered my system, it would have depressed my respiratory drive and likely would have killed me. It turns out that combat gauze saved my life in more ways than one. Miracle.

The afternoon of my injury, Sunday, November 21, I hopped from one base to the next as I inched my way toward Germany. First I was flown to Camp Bastion, where I was treated by an Army Forward

Surgical Team. My official ruling upon arrival was PEA (pulseless electrical activity), meaning I had flatlined, but the medical staff there restarted my heart and managed to stabilize me enough to send me on to Kandahar, a short flight away, at approximately 5:30 P.M. There, I underwent several surgeries over three days, including a seven-hour operation to remove the shrapnel from my skull and brain; the surgeons also did some preliminary work on my right eye socket. From Kandahar, I was flown to Bagram Air Base, the largest U.S. base in Afghanistan, and from Bagram, thirty-two hundred miles to Ramstein Air Base in southwestern Germany on the morning of November 24. Somewhere in there I flatlined again and was revived a second time.

Miracle.

GILBERT, SOUTH CAROLINA
Monday, November 22, 2010

My parents stared at the computer screen, eager but scared to open the email. They had been obsessively calling the number Gunny Tart had given them every thirty minutes since yesterday, but there was no update. Now, they had an official-looking message in their in-box.

******* CASUALTY REPORT *******

****

Report Type: INIT

Casualty Type: Hostile

Casualty Status: VSI ILL/INJURY

Casualty Category: Wounded In Action

Last Name: CARPENTER

First Name: WILLIAM

Middle Name: K

Service: United States Marine Corps

Military Rank: LCPL

Military Unit of Assignment: 2/9, RCT-1, 1ST MARDIV

(FWD), I MEF (FWD)

(PARENT CMD: 2D MARDIV)

Date/Time of Incident (New/Old): 20101121/1130

Inflicting Force: Enemy Forces

Incident City: HELMAND PROVINCE

Incident Country: Afghanistan

Circumstance: LCPL CARPENTER WAS STRUCK BY
FRAGMENTATION TO THE NECK, RIGHT HIP, RIGHT
THIGH, RIGHT FOOT, AND LEFT SIDE OF THE CHEST
CAUSING A RIGHT SIDE PNEUMOTHORAX WHILE
CONDUCTING COMBAT OPERATIONS AGAINST ENEMY

FORCES IN HELMAND PROVINCE, AFGHANISTAN. LCPL CARPENTER WAS PARTICIPATING IN PARTNERED DISMOUNTED STATIC SECURITY OPERATIONS WHEN HE RECEIVED WOUNDS FROM AN ENEMY HAND GRENADE EXPLOSION. LCPL CARPENTER WAS TREATED ON SCENE BY COMPETENT MEDICAL AUTHORITY AND WAS MEDEVAC'D TO THE CAMP BASTION ROLE III MEDICAL FACILITY FOR FURTHER MEDICAL TREATMENT.

SSGT KROLL, PLATOON SERGEANT, WAS THE SENIOR MAN ON SCENE AND IDENTIFIED LCPL CARPENTER BY MEANS OF PERSONAL ASSOCIATION. LCPL CARPENTER WAS WEARING THE NEW KEVLAR HELMET, BALLISTIC EYE-WEAR, NOMEX GLOVES, SCALABLE PLATE CARRIER WITH FRONT AND BACK ESAPI PLATES AND TWO SIDE ESAPI PLATES. (MM: 11-21D)

Diagnosis Info: PENETRATING FRAGMENTATION WOUNDS TO THE LEFT SIDE OF THE CHEST, NECK, RIGHT HIP, RIGHT THIGH, RIGHT FOOT, AND A RIGHT SIDE PNEUMOTHORAX

Progress Report: Report Date: 20101121 Hospital: CAMP BASTION ROLE III MEDICAL TREATMENT FACILITY City: CAMP BASTION Country: AF

Remarks: THE BATTALION SURGEON AND THE COMMANDING OFFICER CONCUR THAT LCPL CARPENTER SUSTAINED HIS INJURIES IN THE LINE OF DUTY AND DUE TO ENEMY ACTION. THE PROPER MEDICAL AUTHORITIES WILL MAKE THE APPROPRIATE ENTRIES IN LCPL CARPENTER'S MEDICAL RECORD. NOK HAS NOT BEEN NOTIFIED.
THE MARINE IS MALE AND HIS MOS IS 0311.
SUPP
PCR WILL FOLLOW AS NECESSARY.

The memo offered relief mingled with horror. They had tried to remind each other that a combat injury could be something as relatively minor as collateral shrapnel but they also knew it could be devastating: wounding by sniper fire, a suicide bomb, an IED.

Or a grenade.

Now they knew that my injury was on the "catastrophic" end of the spectrum. But at least they also knew I had survived the night. But how much longer could I hang on?

My parents reached out to anyone and everyone they knew who might be able to give them further information or connect them with someone who could. Finally, regular reports began to trickle in so that they at least knew where I was. As soon as they received word that I was headed to Germany, they started making plans in case they needed to travel there to be with me. My mother was desperate for that call, desperate to see me. What they didn't know at the time is that the military only sends families to Germany when they don't believe the patient will survive long enough to be transported back to the States. So my parents kept waiting hopefully by the phone. Mom told me that every hour felt like a week. And she began researching flights on her own.

Finally, they were alerted that I would be arriving at the National Naval Medical Center in Bethesda, Maryland, on Friday, November 26. They packed up their bags, dropped our dog Sadie off with a friend, and then drove to my dad's aunt's house in Richmond, Virginia. Richmond is about 120 miles south of Bethesda, a straight shot up I-95. It was Thanksgiving, but they simply couldn't stay in the house any longer. At least driving north felt like they were making some kind of progress toward being reunited as a family.

LANDSTUHL REGIONAL MEDICAL CENTER: SOUTHWESTERN GERMANY
Wednesday, November 24, 2010

After the nine-to-ten-hour flight from Bagram to Ramstein, we were loaded onto medical buses—which are essentially just school buses refurbished to hold anywhere between 10 and 25 patients—for a 10-minute ride through the mountains to Landstuhl Regional Medical Center (LRMC), the largest American military hospital in Europe. It serves both American and coalition forces wounded in combat in the Middle East and Central Asia, as well as providing specialized care for American service members and their families stationed in the region. Landstuhl has the nickname "Halfway Home," because once wounded military members make it there, their chances of survival rise drastically. The fact that I had survived long enough to make it to Landstuhl was . . . a miracle.

As you might imagine, any hospital that enormous has a large and dedicated chaplain corps. At Landstuhl, each branch of the service had two chaplains and two assistants to serve their soldiers, Marines, sailors, and airmen, plus a number of other coalition countries had chaplains on staff, too. Each day, the chaplains were briefed on the flights coming in and who was aboard. They received word when the buses left Ramstein and waited to meet each one as it pulled up so that they could personally greet every single service member being unloaded, conscious or not. The ones who can walk are taken to an intake room for a brief introduction; the ones who can't are wheeled inside, either into a room for evaluation or straight into the ICU for further surgeries. But each stretcher stops for the chaplain, who introduces himself or herself and says a short prayer for the individual. It takes only a few moments, but is an important part of respecting the humanity of every service member.

On Wednesday, November 24, Master Sergeant Chuck Williams, a chaplain's assistant from South Carolina, was reviewing the list of "chalks" (inbound flights with new patients) expected that day. He always checked for Reservists and National Guardsmen, since he served through the South Carolina Air National Guard, but that day he was also scanning the lists for my name. He'd gotten a call that there was a critically injured young man from South Carolina arriving, and he thought it might be nice for the Marine to hear a familiar accent praying at his bedside.

It had already been dark for quite some time when the plane landed and we were loaded onto stretchers destined for Landstuhl. Germany in November is a gloomy place—cold and rainy days with late sunrises and early sunsets due to the northern latitude. It was a chilly wait for the chaplains as they stood ready to meet our bus, just as they did multiple times a day. MSGT Williams had made sure that he was part of the group assigned to my flight's arrival, and he was ready to move the moment he heard my name called as I was unloaded and rolled toward the door.

"Hello, Kyle. I'm Chaplain Williams, and I am here to help you with anything you need while you are at Landstuhl," he said gently, leaning down next to my face. Then he spoke a quick prayer for me, and I was whisked away to the operating room.

The next morning, he came into my room to talk with me again—what the chaplain corps calls ministry of presence. I wasn't awake and couldn't ask him any questions or seek his counsel on spiritual matters, but he would sit with me so that I was not alone as I fought for my life. What shocked him most was how swollen and bloated I was from all the internal injuries. He saw shrapnel wounds and broken limbs all the time, and those were terrible enough, but even someone who had never seen me healthy could tell that my body was mangled beyond anything imaginable.

Chaplain Williams settled into the chair next to

my bed and introduced himself again. "I know you don't know me, but I'm from Chapin, which is right across Lake Murray from Lexington. Our towns are on opposite sides of the city. Isn't that just amazing that God put two guys from the exact same area right here together in Germany?" The only sound was the continued beeping of my heart monitor and the whirl and click of the various other machines that were helping to keep me alive. He'd heard that my survival was still tenuous, and given my unresponsiveness, he feared the worst. He prayed for my recovery and my family. He spoke encouraging words to me. And then he started in on the one thing that he knew would strike a chord with every Southerner: football. "I don't know if you're a Gamecock or a Clemson fan—I've got one kid headed to each one so I guess we're a house divided—but I know you want to stick around for another football season. I imagine you probably didn't get to watch any games this fall, but let me tell you that it's been quite a year . . ." And somewhere in the midst of his breakdown of each team's season, I twitched. It was a simple movement but for Chaplain Williams, who was looking for any symbol of hope, that little twitch meant the world. It meant that my brain and body were still communicating, no matter how tenuous the connection might be at the moment, and *that* meant that there was still a chance I would pull through. It was Thanksgiving Day and he was missing his family terribly, but in that moment, he said God gave him a reminder as to why he was there and why the ministry of presence mattered. My little twitch was the thing he was most thankful for that day.

The surgeons, physicians, and nurses at LRMC took the best imaginable care of me. The goal there is to move wounded patients through as quickly as is safe, in order to get them on the next plane back to the United States. Rotator flights, as they are called, departed every Friday, Sunday, and Tuesday, and since I arrived late on Wednesday, the goal was to stabilize me enough to depart on the Friday flight to Bethesda. My family was informed to expect me Friday, and they had started to make plans accordingly. However, my departure was delayed due to blood clots. It is unsafe for anyone to fly with a clot when otherwise healthy; in my condition, it was even more dangerous. As a result, I was held up at Landstuhl.

One of my nurses knew my family would be deeply disappointed by the delay, and he came up with a brilliant solution. Dialing my parents on his cell phone, he held the receiver up to my ear. My mom's voice came on first, then she, Dad, and my brothers all joined in as they passed the phone around the table and told me they loved me and couldn't wait for me to come home. The medical staff in Germany later confirmed that all my vitals leapt at the sound of their voices. My heart rate, my brain activity—everything that had been dangerously low suddenly surged. I may not have been aware of anything around me, but my mind still knew my family's voices. It was the most life anyone had seen from me since I'd arrived. My heart, which had already stopped twice, was now beating as if it had every reason in the world not to quit again.

That phone call helped calm my parents' fears about my being alone. Not only were a steady stream of nurses and Chaplain Williams tending to me, there was also a wonderful woman named Tawny Campbell who made sure that I and other injured guys like me were looked after and loved as we were being put back together by the surgeons.

On Tuesday morning, Tawny had received an email from a friend who mentioned a family with a newly injured son, and he might be headed to Landstuhl. Tawny and her family were stationed in Germany, and Tawny's husband was an Army flight medic deployed in Helmand Province at the same time I was. Together with her young daughters, she was a regular fixture at LRMC, visiting wounded soldiers and Marines and making "Angel Bags" with snacks, toiletries, and a few goodies to give to the guys before they departed for the U.S. Her friend figured that if anyone could get in to check on me and report back, it was Tawny. Tawny connected with my mom, got some basic information, and started making inquiries.

On the afternoon of Thanksgiving, when I'd been at Landstuhl less than twenty-four hours, Tawny got permission to visit me in the ICU. With one of her daughters sitting cross-legged outside my door with a coloring book, Tawny came quietly into my room and touched my unbandaged left hand. She introduced herself, making mental notes of how to describe me to my parents; even though I didn't look as bad off as many of the other guys she had seen, my mouth and tongue were horribly swollen, and she knew there had to be extensive internal injuries to be causing that. Tawny started telling me about the Thanksgiving meal she had just had downstairs in the dining hall, with her daughters going from table to table asking, "Are you a hurt soldier? May I sit with you?" She knew I couldn't hear her, but she wanted to make some sort of a human connection anyway. She described the way the place was decorated and the food they had served. And then, suddenly, just as had happened with the chaplain that morning, I made a small movement. It was just a flexing of my fingers—almost as if I was stretching them under the gentle pressure of her hand—but it was unmistakable. "You're still here," she whispered.

Tawny stayed for about twenty minutes, then went home and emailed my family a full report. She also used her investigative skills that she had honed working as a journalist for a number of years, and went through my mom's Facebook page, looking for any pictures, stories, or names that she could use to talk with me in a more personal way—anything to touch part of my mind if I happened to jolt into consciousness while she was there the next day. She didn't have a whole lot to go on, but she wove together a loose story line about my brothers and what they might be doing back home in South Carolina. The following evening, after I got out of hours-long surgery on my skull, face, and jaw, she told it to me, describing little details and saying the names Price and Peyton, Peyton and Price, as often as she could in the hopes that somewhere in my mind, wherever I was at the time, I could hear her and be reminded of home, safety, and the people I loved.

By Saturday, it looked like the blood clot issue was resolving and I would be able to make it onto the Sunday flight to Bethesda. The swelling had started to go down in my face, which made the burn marks from the grenade more apparent. But the surgeons had stitched up some of the open wounds, and she could see on my upper lip that I needed to shave. These were all details she fired off to my parents in another email to help reassure them that there was enough of my face left to grow a tiny mustache. She also snapped some photos so my folks could get a sense of what I looked like, so that their initial sight of me wouldn't shock them quite as much. Now I had burn ointment on my face, which is the consistency of petroleum jelly but bright pink, and makes you look like your face is melting off. This, she assured them, was just the medicine, not the state of my skin.

"Keep strong," she wrote. "Your boy is coming home."

On Sunday, November 28, I was cleared to head home. As it turned out, however, mine was not a typical flight. There was an Army sniper on board named Ryan Craig, whose mother, Jennifer Miller, was a nurse. Ryan had taken a bullet to the head in a firefight, and his chances of survival had been set even lower than mine. Jennifer had received the dreaded invitation from the military to come over to Germany to say goodbye to her son, but by the time she arrived, his condition had begun to improve and suddenly, it looked like he was going to survive after all. Like me, Ryan was still unconscious, but he, too, had been cleared to fly back home. As she settled in next to him for the trip, Jennifer heard me start to make a sound. My bed was next to Ryan's, and as she listened, she realized I was saying "Mom." She knew immediately what she had to do—what any mother would do. She situated herself right between us, and with one hand she reached out to her son, and with her other hand, she reached out to me. She held his hand *and* my hand the entire eight-hour flight.

In her email exchanges with Tawny earlier in the week, my mom had remarked on how grateful the family was for everyone who was lifting up my healing and my body in prayer. "When that body heals," Mom wrote, "he will know what a miracle he is."

But I didn't need to wait for healing. The miracle was already unfolding, one stranger after another, who went to extraordinary lengths to be there for an injured Marine who was finally headed home.

NATIONAL NAVAL MEDICAL CENTER: BETHESDA, MARYLAND
Sunday, November 28, 2010

My family drove straight to the hospital from Richmond; they didn't even stop at the Navy Lodge—the hotel on base—to check in and drop off their bags.

There were still several hours before my plane was slated to land, but I think my mom was panicking that we might touch down way ahead of schedule and they would miss my arrival—and there was no way on earth Robin Carpenter was going to allow her injured boy to make a seven-thousand-mile journey home and not have familiar faces there to greet him.

They were met by a doctor and a chaplain who explained a bit more about my condition and what would happen when I arrived: I would be rolled in quickly, with just a moment or two for them to see me in the waiting area before I had to be taken back to have my condition reassessed; then it would be straight to the ICU. They would be able to sit and talk to me later, but the most pressing matter at the moment was getting me the medical care I needed as quickly as possible. Of course they all agreed.

My family went to the designated waiting area, near the flags at the entrance, which had become a holding station for families who were there to meet rotator flights. Price remarked later how strange it was to be in a hospital that felt so empty. Obviously, other floors and wards were bustling with combat injuries, but on the Sunday after Thanksgiving, the waiting area was pretty quiet. There was just one other family there, and my mom struck up a conversation with the other mom; I think worried mothers have an automatic bond over their shared fears for their children. But everyone just made a little small talk because no one was feeling especially social, given the reason they were all there.

Nick had arrived at Bethesda a few days earlier on a different rotator flight, and while my family was waiting for me, they ran into Nick's girlfriend and Tiffany Aguiar, one of his best friends from childhood. Tiffany was in college at George Washington University and had taken the Metro over to Bethesda to see Nick. The two women were leaving the hospital for the evening when they recognized my family and decided to wait with them for my arrival.

Finally, sometime after sunset, they got word that our flight was touching down. A few minutes later they heard that the bus was coming in from the airfield. At that point, it was as if everyone just came out of the shadows. Suddenly, the quiet waiting area was flooded with nearly a dozen doctors and nurses, ready to whisk the new arrivals away to the ICU operating room.

The first bed came off the bus—it was Ryan. The chaplain stepped forward, Ryan's name was announced, and four or five people in scrubs and white coats descended, rolling his bed straight ahead and down the hall to wherever they needed to take him. Jennifer ran alongside his bed before heading up to the ICU waiting room.

It was my turn next as the well-practiced pattern was repeated: off the bus, chaplain prays, name announced, medical crew pounces, bed rolls. The way I was bandaged, my face was visible, but it was so banged up that I'm sure I wasn't recognizable. I had a homemade, patriotic quilt tucked around me for warmth—it must have been something donated to the hospital at Landstuhl. The only uncovered part of me was a little two-inch section on my left leg. A doctor stopped my bed for just a minute and told my family they could safely touch me there. My brothers hung back and let my parents step forward. Mom reached out her hand and made contact for just a moment, then the bed started rolling again and she began running alongside it, trying to keep up, reassuring me that I was home and the whole family was there and I was going to be okay and everyone loved me so much . . .

And then I disappeared onto the elevator.

But if my vital signs had shown I registered my family's voices over the phone, I can only imagine how much greater the response was to hearing their voices in person and actually feeling my mother's touch. The doctors hadn't been sure I was going to make it, but my family had been. And that unshakable belief had registered with my body and brain.

Like I said, there are two types of miracles. The care, attention, and dedication shown to me by the incredible medical staff all along the way—from the rooftop, to the combat hospitals at Bastion, Kandahar, and Bagram, to Landstuhl, to my arrival, at last, at Bethesda—were all part of that second miracle. The kindness and humanity shown to me by all of the people who went above and beyond to make sure I was not alone were also part of that miracle. Even though I remember none of it, it is an essential and indelible part of my story. People can be miracles for one another; that is one of the greatest and most sustaining lessons I have learned in my life and some of the best advice I can offer to anyone else: Be part of someone else's miracle.

That, and call your mom.

Chapter 9
Find the Joy

Grief affects everyone differently. It is deeply personal, but also deeply relational. You are internally facing your own emotions of fear and loss, but the source of grief is a connection with another person, which means that your emotion is also directed outward. My parents, ever the perfect team, found that their grief complemented each other's.

From the moment my family received news of my injury, my dad was the anchor. He remained calm, measured, and tried to keep his emotions in check while he dealt with the basic work of sorting out what needed to be done. He made the phone calls, the travel plans, the hotel reservations. He was able to maintain control of his emotions to make sure the family all made it to Bethesda. He also knew he had to stay strong for my mom, who was absolutely distraught. Dad held everyone together.

The moment I was wheeled into Bethesda and my family was able to see me, however, the roles reversed. It was as if all of the calm, rational energy that my dad had been able to muster to get my mom and brothers to that point evaporated the moment he came face-to-face with the real extent of my injuries. My mother, however, tapped into a reserve of strength that amazed everyone.

As soon as my initial assessment in ICU was finished and my family was admitted to my room, my dad's knees buckled. A nurse had to help him out of the room, then he just sank down, curled up, and couldn't talk. The last thing he recalls seeing before he left was my mom grabbing the rails on the bed and climbing carefully up so she could be right next to my face to talk to me. While I was still across the ocean, she had been a mess, but the moment I was back on home soil and she could see me, her "mama bear" instinct took over and she was afraid of nothing. Every day I was in Afghanistan, my mom had been sure I was going to die. She was terrified to turn on the news, even though she knew next of kin would be informed before anything was released to the media. She had lived in a constant state of dread that at any minute, a uniformed officer would be at the door to state his regrets. But the moment I touched down in the States, all of that fear disappeared. For the entirety of my deployment she was absolutely sure she was going to be burying me from Afghanistan. But she never worried she was going to bury me from Bethesda. The moment she got to lay eyes on me, she never had another concern that I wasn't going to survive. She confessed later that she had resolved to will me to live. "I know that sounds crazy," she admitted. "But I thought, 'I'm your mom. I carried you for nine months and gave you life. If I can be near you, I can make sure you are taken care of right, and that means you *will* survive this.'" And that optimism, combined with her faith that God wasn't done with me yet, powered her through the difficult weeks and months ahead.

My brothers waited outside the ICU until our parents had a chance to see me, then Dad managed to collect himself enough to go get them, and Mom ushered them in. The room was dimly lit and filled with machines that were helping me breathe, feeding me, and monitoring my vitals. The only bits of me that weren't covered with bandages were that three-inch spot on my lower left leg and now, part of my left cheek. Price and Peyton each took a turn sliding one finger along my cheek and saying hello. Peyton remarked later that the first impression wasn't pretty, but there was an incredible sense of reassurance now that he could see me with his own eyes and confirm that I really was alive. It was a good moment, he said, but a hard one.

As Dad waited for my brothers to come back out, Mom settled in next to my bed and didn't move for the next two days. Finally, on Wednesday, she went to my dad and told him he had to come in and see me. When my dad insisted it was too much to take, Mom refused to accept that.

"He knows we're there, Jim," she insisted. "When I talk to him, his heart rate starts to rise. He needs you there."

So my dad prayed for courage, got up the nerve, and went back to my room. He struggled at first to speak, then finally managed to choke out, "Hey, son." Sure enough, my heart monitor registered an increase. That was all he needed. He reached for the unbandaged spot just above my left foot, and then all the words he'd held in the past few days came pouring out: "I'm here, son. It's going to be okay. We're all here and we love you. You're going to be all right—I promise." He rubbed that ankle raw.

My surgeries were scheduled for every other day or every third day, depending on the procedure. One of the most pressing needs was for my wounds to be washed and redressed every forty-eight hours in order to avoid infection, but I also had to undergo multiple procedures to try to repair my jaw and few remaining teeth, my skull fracture, and the multiplicity of other injuries that were keeping me in critical condition. My right eye was gone—there had been no way to salvage it—but my left eye was still working, incredibly. My right arm was fractured in thirty places; there didn't seem to be much hope of saving it, either, and my parents were concerned about what that would mean for my future, since I am right-handed.

Just ahead of the surgery on my arm, my parents were sitting in the waiting room when the surgeon, Dr. Newman, came out to meet them. My mom took a deep breath as she shook his hand and cut to the chase: "Well, they prepared us for amputation."

Dr. Newman pulled his head back incredulously and said, "Amputation? We're not amputating that arm. We're gonna *save* that arm." That was the first glimmer of hope they had that maybe my long-term prognosis wouldn't be quite as devastating as they had imagined. Dr. Newman had studied my charts, my X-rays, and me, and as delicate a procedure as it was going to be, he knew he was up to the challenge . . . and he was right. It took thirteen hours and several surgeries to restore my arm to functionality, and it was still fragile for more than a year afterward, but thanks to Dr. Newman's incredible skill and dedication, I didn't lose it. Things were looking up.

Once they had seen that I was home and going to make it—the survival rate for combat-wounded personnel is around 98 percent once they reach Bethesda—my brothers had to get home to South Carolina. They were in their freshman year of high school, and couldn't stay out of school indefinitely. Friends and relatives took turns staying with them while my parents remained at Bethesda with me. I am still in awe of my little brothers and the burden they carried during that time. Never once did Price or Peyton question whether it was fair that our parents' attention was focused on me at the moment; even when my parents had to miss their fifteenth birthdays less than two weeks after my injury, they didn't complain. I can't imagine how the disruption and uncertainty must have affected them, but they handled it with more maturity and understanding than any other teenagers I can imagine. And the people in our community who stepped in at that time to be family for my brothers gave us a gift we can never repay.

After Price and Peyton flew home, my parents' time consisted of sitting with me, then grabbing some rest and maybe a shower while I was in surgery for eight or more hours a day. I think having my brothers there had kept them occupied, so now Mom channeled her energy into updating the Facebook page called "Operation Kyle." It was something my parents' Sunday school class had started a few weeks previously as part of an effort to ship my unit Christmas presents; now, it was a place for updates and prayer requests, and just a connection to the outside world while my parents remained sequestered in the ICU. Mom updated it almost every day; the rest of the time they spent praying and researching how to navigate the military health-care system.

My parents were introduced to Janine Canty, my caseworker through the Semper Fi Fund (SFF), which exists to provide support to injured service members and their families in a variety of ways. When Janine saw that my mom didn't have a jacket (in her panicked state, she forgot to pack one), she got her one. In fact, black fleece SFF jackets were a pretty common sight at Bethesda in those days. It was a simple gesture, but the first of a hundred needs, big and small, that Janine and SFF would help to meet in the coming years.

By the end of that first week at Bethesda, I was apparently awake and alert—I would follow people with my eye and blink and nod in response to questions—

but I was not yet talking, other than some groans and incoherent mumbling. My first memory is from about a week after that, when I opened my eye and saw hospital equipment. It was weird, because the last thing I could recall clearly was being on that rooftop in Afghanistan. I was definitely disoriented now, but in my confusion, I just rolled with it. Gradually, a seated figure next to me came into focus, and I managed to croak out the words "Hey, Dad."

My parents were ecstatic. Not only was I awake and talking, but I seemed to have enough of my memory still intact that I could recognize my father. That was the main thing they had been praying for: If my body was destroyed, they could adapt; but if my brain had been affected so that I was no longer myself, that was the outcome they feared most. I don't remember much else again for a few more days, but that simple statement of "Hey, Dad" was the first glimpse of hope for my family that I might still be me—at least partially.

I'm not going to lie: It was difficult as I slowly became cognizant of the extent of my injuries. I think it was difficult for my parents to watch, too, as I gradually started to realize one thing after another, each time I emerged back into consciousness.

I've lost an eye.

I've woken up with no teeth.

I can't feel my face.

I can't lift my arms.

But once reality sunk in, I didn't enter any kind of deep mourning period for my body or my old life—at least, not yet. The more aware I became of the extent of my injuries, the more I realized what a miracle it was that I was alive at all. Maybe my tendency to compete with myself kicked in right away; maybe my mom was right and she really was willing me to live. Whatever the case, my focus quickly switched from the injuries that were out of my control to whatever recovery and rehab I could do to maximize the facilities I still had. I don't think people believed at first that my positive perspective was genuine; I'm pretty sure my family and nurses thought I was in denial or not fully lucid. But I was driven by three things. The first was the simple fact that I couldn't undo my injuries. Second, I had a desire to be strong for everyone around me who was clearly struggling with how to support me. Finally, I was motivated not to let my injuries and, by extension, the Taliban have any power over me—for the sake of every Marine who had gone before me, and those still fighting.

On December 11, I made a big move up to the mythical fifth floor—a room *outside* of the ICU. Less than three weeks after falling on a grenade, I was stable enough to be moved to a "normal" hospital room. It seemed too good to be true.

It was.

I am standing on top of a small hill looking down and across a field, watching a funeral. The sky is so gray it almost seems more dark than light. There are no tombstones, not even at the gravesite of the person being buried. The only person in attendance is the pastor, who is holding the Bible and standing at the head of the grave. I begin to wonder why I am here, standing on this hill by myself. As the pastor begins to speak, I realize the horrifying answer to my question: I am watching my own funeral, and no one has come. The Marines I had called my brothers were so disappointed that I left them behind in Afghanistan that they didn't come to say goodbye. I try to yell out, but I can't. I try to take a step, but I can't. I am paralyzed with despair as tears roll down my face.

I was started on a new painkiller that night, and I did not respond well. To this day, I don't know if it was the medicine itself or the dosage, but something about it did not interact well with my body.

I am lying in bed. My heart races as I try to process how they got into the hospital. I am fixated on what used to be the silver sprinkler heads that are mounted in ceilings. Now, they are bullet holes. They have been shot out by the Taliban, who have taken over the hospital and are now in the room above mine unloading AK-47 rounds down into my room. I can't move as my mom stays at my bedside with me. She gets shot in the leg, and I have never felt so helpless. The shooting suddenly stops. Seconds later, the silence is interrupted by the dreaded clinking of a hand grenade bouncing on my hospital room floor. The Taliban dropped it down through one of the holes in the roof and it lands at the foot of my bed. I hear the nurse scream, "No! He has been through enough already!" She jumps on it. I watch the pink mist and body parts that are the only things left of her float around my room.

My parents told me later that night was the worst of their life—even worse than getting the call I'd been injured or seeing my mangled body when I'd arrived. Up to that point, I had still been Kyle—just physically battered Kyle. They had no idea who this hallucinating person was, and I was so far gone to wherever my mind had taken me, they were afraid they would never get me back.

I was returned to ICU early the next morning.

My dad, frantic that our family can't afford my medical bills, loads himself down with weapons and storms the emergency room to demand that I get the surgeries I need and to reverse the hospital's order to discharge me. I try to scream and beg him not to. I want to tell him it's okay and that he doesn't have to do this, even if I can't get any more care. As the second set of the ICU sliding doors open, he is met by a SWAT team, who unload on him until I see him fall behind the nurses' station. The last thing I remember is the sound of the shotgun my dad was holding as it hits the ground. I think about how much he must have loved me to do something like that.

For the next several days, whenever I woke up and saw my dad sitting in a chair in the corner of my room, I was shocked that he was alive. No one could have lived through what I had just seen happen to him.

From the corner of my eye I see something dark, like a shadow, moving on the floor near my bed. I am completely gripped with fear and unable to move. As more of them start crawling down the walls, I realize my room is being flooded with giant spiders. They climb over each other, try to scurry up on my bed. They are so big that their hairs resemble long, black human hair. They are so heavy that I can feel the tug of my bedsheets as their horrible legs grapple to get a foothold to climb up onto me. The first one to me stands on my chest and pauses for a moment. Saliva drips from its fangs as it stares into my eyes. Suddenly, like a horse, it raises up on its hind legs and falls forward, clamping its fangs down on my throat.

The hallucinations were intense. At no point did it ever occur to me that the things I was seeing, hearing, and feeling might all be in my head. Every detail was so vivid and lifelike. To this day, they are forever locked in my brain not as memories of hallucinations I had, but as memories of real events I experienced.

Both of my arms have been amputated and my new prosthetics are wooden sticks. Just like on a snowman, they are long, thin, and have two forks at the end. It is time for me to move to a new hospital, so I ask for my sticks to be attached for the journey. Then suddenly, I am standing in the back of a cargo plane. Oddly, there are no seats, no flight crew, and nothing to even hold on to. Where are my machines and medical equipment? Perhaps the doctors sent them separately to the new hospital. As we fly over Atlanta, we bank suddenly to the right. The only thing in the back of the plane is a big red button—almost cartoonish—on the wall. As we continue the hard turn, I lose my balance. When I try to brace my stick arm against the wall, I accidentally hit the button. The engines shut off and my stomach drops as we fall from the sky. As we plummet toward the ground, I can see that we were headed straight for Turner Field, the old home of the Atlanta Braves. I can't help but think, in a weirdly calm and logical manner, how strange it is that I am going to ac-

cidentally crash a plane into a place where I loved to visit and watch games growing up.

Because my mind was so thoroughly convinced of what was happening, elements of the imaginary crept into my cognition when I was alert. I would ask repeatedly for my "sticks" when I needed to reach for something, believing that I had to have the wooden snowman arms inserted into my shoulders. Even once my parents were able to assure me that my dad really was alive, I remained convinced that he had been blown away by that SWAT team and was suspicious of the person now claiming to be him. I imagined the same thing about my mom. "Show me your legs, Mom," I would insist. "I know you were shot." I knew she was lying to protect me but it made me angry every time she told me she hadn't been shot. They would reassure me that everything was fine, but even then I wasn't convinced.

In the corner of my room, there is a red-haired girl hanging from my ceiling. She is extremely pale. Her hair is hanging down, her eyes are both beautiful and terrifyingly blue, and covered in a glossy layer, and her neck is bruised. Everyone tries to tell me it is just the red Marine Corps flag that is set up in the corner of my room, but I know what I see. She doesn't do anything— just stands there and stares at me with her face slightly contorted, not dead but not blinking.

I lie in bed, listening in horror as my parents speak with my doctor outside of my hospital room. The door is slightly cracked, and I can hear them talking but it's difficult for me to comprehend what I am hearing. My parents are telling my doctor to "just go ahead and take him off life support." I can hear the faint but continuous flatline sound of my heart-rate monitor in the background. I scream out again and again, pleading for them not to do this. It is hard to breathe but I use everything I have to make them hear me. Then my last bit of will to live leaves me as I realize they want this to happen. They are too emotionally worn down to continue going through this. I start to fade away as the chaplain walks into my room and the staff starts unplugging all of my machines.

By mid-December, I was gradually coming back to myself, more able to discern between waking and dreaming, and more able to retain information about what had happened to me so that I was not confused each time I awoke. The hallucinations began to fade, though I was still convinced from time to time that there was someone behind my bed, messing with my machines. I would make my dad (with his miraculously restored body) go back and check for me, even though he could obviously see that no one was there.

As my lucidity returned, so did my awareness of

basic wants and needs, as well as my curiosity. I asked for a mirror, a request my mom had been dreading because she was not sure how I would react. As she held one up, I studied the scars that crisscrossed my face. It was a lot to take in. I didn't say anything at first, so my mom cautiously pointed out that I had grown a mustache while I'd been in a coma. "I'm going to need to shave," I said, finally.

Mom laughed. "Definitely before they award you your Purple Heart."

"I'd rather have a cold tropical drink right now than a Purple Heart," I cracked, only half joking.

I had been on a feeding tube for close to a month, and as I became increasingly conscious of my surroundings, I began to miss the taste of things. I had to undergo what is called a swallow study to confirm that my throat was functioning, and strong enough for me to be able to consume anything independent of my tube, given the state of my jaw and neck, and all the surgeries I had recently undergone. A few days after my hallucinations ended, I finally passed it. My reward was that I was allowed to drink liquids on my own. I can't begin to explain how thirsty I felt after almost a month of having liquids pumped into my body but nothing passing through my lips. There is something "rehumanizing" about being able to consume food again after a major injury. It would be several more weeks before I would be able to start eating real food, but just being able to state a preference for something and then taste it was amazing—the sort of thing you don't realize you take for granted every day. In fact, I was so happy about this milestone that my mom updated the Operation Kyle Facebook page on December 14 with this note: *Kyle passed his swallow test today and was able to have water, Gatorade, and Sprite! I'm not sure if we have ever seen him so happy. In his own words, "It has been an excellent day."*

The next day I managed to sit in a chair before being transferred back up to the fifth floor. By that evening, I was out of intensive care for good and sipping a chocolate protein shake for dinner. My mom hung colored Christmas lights and five stockings for my family, and waking up to that sight was one of the first really solid memories I had in the hospital. It helped me feel anchored in a time and place.

When winter break started, my brothers came back to Bethesda so we could spend Christmas together as a family. On Christmas Eve, my family rode the Metro to Best Buy. Price and Peyton picked out laptops and my dad got my mom a digital camera. I think it may have been the first time since I arrived that she left the hospital to do more than shower or grab a quick bite to eat. When they got back to the hospital, my mom asked me if she could take photos to start documenting my recovery. I agreed, apparently, but as she admits, "It probably would not be admissible in court."

My surgeries continued on an every-other-day basis, and every procedure left me more in awe of what my health-care team was capable of. They all commented on how amazing my improvement was, but the fact is, they were making it possible. With every procedure, they were restoring or reconstructing or renewing my body in some way to help make me as independent and self-sufficient as possible. I can't imagine what it must have been like for them to spend eight or nine hours in the operating room, working on something like wiring together the remnants of my jaw or grafting skin from my legs to transplant elsewhere on my body. They worked tirelessly and with complete focus, and on the days when I wasn't in surgery, they were giving the same tremendous care to the other injured service members who were there. My parents tried to make a point of expressing their gratitude to the doctors, nurses, and staff, and the response was almost always along the lines of "No, it's my privilege to care for your son."

What impressed me even more was the care that the staff at Bethesda managed to give every patient at a time when they were vastly overworked. The hospital was slammed—so many casualties were coming in weekly at the end of 2010 and in early 2011 that they briefly ran out of rooms and had hospital beds lining the halls. A new, expanded facility was being built at the time that would have more room and merge operations and resources with Walter Reed Army Medical Center, but it was still about nine months from completion and demand was outpacing the rate of construction.

On Christmas, I cracked myself up by asking every nurse or doctor who came into the room if they knew what they were doing. Obviously, the fact that I was alive was evidence of that, but the simpler the task, the funnier it was to me to ask. If a nurse was changing a drip bag or checking my vitals, I would look highly concerned before saying, "Are you sure you know what you're doing?" If a doctor gave me a detailed rundown on the next procedure, explaining every complex element of it in fancy medical terms, I would nod and look like I understood every word. When they asked if I had any questions, I would say, "Yes, I have one: Are you sure you know what you're doing?" and then start laughing hysterically. I had been out of practice for a month, so my humor was a little rusty, but it sure felt good to laugh.

On December 30, General James F. Amos, Commandant of the Marine Corps, and Sergeant Major of the Marine Corps Carlton Kent visited Bethesda and awarded me the Purple Heart right there in my hospital room. It was impossible to get a shirt on me because my arms were still severely damaged and covered in tubes and bandages. So they placed the medal directly on my chest as I laid in the bed. Despite my big words a week or two earlier, I definitely would *not* trade that moment for a tropical drink.

What was even better than the Purple Heart, however, was another response that the Commandant's visit elicited. Nick had taken a piece of shrapnel to the forehead, just under the rim of his helmet, and had been unconscious most of his time in the hospital. He received the Purple Heart as well, and as the Commandant and Sergeant Major made another round of visits, they stopped in his room. Tiffany Aguiar was there, visiting Nick at the time, and shared with General Amos how Nick had inspired her to do NROTC so she could be a Marine officer after college. She explained what an inspiring individual he was, both as a person and as a Marine, and that even though he had been pretty unresponsive so far, she was hopeful that if she kept talking to him, he would eventually be able to tell that people there cared about him. As the Commandant prepared to leave, he turned to Nick and said in his booming voice, "Hang in there, Marine."

Then, as if he were moving through water, with difficulty but concentrated precision, Nick slowly curled his hand into a fist and popped his trademark thumbs-up.

Tiffany screamed and then started crying. "That's the first thing I've seen him do!" she gasped. Nick Eufrazio, a Marine's Marine, managed while in something like a coma to give a thumbs-up to the Commandant. If ever there was a moment that encapsulated everything that made him special, it was that one.

Besides Nick, there were several other familiar faces in the hospital with me, including Stinson, our former squad leader who had lost his legs to an IED about ten days before my injury. His wife, Tesa, drove back and forth to their home in Pennsylvania as he continued to get treatment and do rehab. Just after the holidays, he was moved to the VA medical center in Richmond, Virginia, but it was nice to get to see him and meet his wife, after hearing him talk so much about her and his concern for her as we waited for his medevac to arrive. Although I obviously wish it could have been under different circumstances, I loved that my family had a chance to meet some of the people I had told them about in my letters home. Jennifer Miller was also there, along with her son Ryan's older brother and sister, to support his recovery. They had plenty of time to talk and connect with my family while Ryan and I were in surgery.

On January 10, 2011 I insisted on staying awake to watch the college football national championship, number-one Auburn versus number-two Oregon. It was quite a feat for me, given that I still had a tendency to fall asleep midsentence when I was talking with someone. But those little moments of normalcy—glimpses of life that had nothing at all to do with the hospital or injuries or rehab or any of that—were wonderful.

I was thrilled when I learned that Nick had woken up. For a variety of reasons, I only saw Nick a couple of times in the hospital, but it made my day when he penned "Wazzup Kyle" on his whiteboard when he was doing occupational therapy for writing. We were just a few rooms apart but still bedridden, so we started sending a whiteboard back and forth with short messages we'd practiced writing to each other. It was encouraging to me to see that Nick was on the same journey I was: We were reclaiming our lives and learning how to be our fullest selves, not in spite of our injuries but because of them. Our injuries happened. Nothing would ever change that. Our wounds were a part of our bodies, but we were the ones who would get to choose what role they would play in our stories.

My dad and brothers had to go back to South Carolina early in January, but Mom stayed with me. I still couldn't eat normally and my sense of taste was almost nonexistent, but the one thing I found I really could enjoy was a vanilla milkshake. There was a McDonald's on base but it was a decent walk from the main building, where we were. As testament to a mother's love, my mom—a Mississippi girl, born and raised— would bundle up every day and walk through the wind, snow, and whatever other awfulness a mid-Atlantic winter could throw at her, in order to get me one. Sometimes she went more than once a day. And she held them for me while I would drink them. My arms were still largely immobile, and I spent most of the day with them resting on my "cheeses," the nickname we gave the wedges on either side of me that helped keep my arms elevated. It was frustrating not being able to do something as basic as hold a milkshake, but I was grateful for my mom's tireless dedication to my care and comfort.

There were times when the PICC line (my IV) wouldn't flow correctly with my pain blockers, or something wasn't healing quite right so that my injuries began to hurt in unimaginable ways, but I found it hard to complain: I had the greatest care in the world, both medically and personally, and I was alive. I couldn't imagine anyone luckier than I was.

JANUARY 2011

By the second week of January, I was stable enough to be transferred to the polytrauma unit at the Richmond VA, but it was actually a lot harder than I had imagined to say goodbye to my health-care team at Bethesda. Of course I was glad that this move meant that my health was continuing to improve, but I had really gotten to know and love the people who were taking such outstanding care of me. Dr. Lauren Turza, my head trauma surgeon, for example, had secured special permission to have us to her home for dinner. Even though my palate was still limited, it was the biggest morale boost just to be able to leave the hospital and do something normal. Bethesda had been good to me, but it was time to make room for the next group of seriously injured guys to receive lifesaving care.

Richmond was so different from Bethesda. For one thing, I went from an extremely overcrowded unit to a much quieter and much emptier hospital. Mom was able to stay at the Richmond Fisher House, a facility provided for the family members of seriously injured or ill service members while their loved ones are in the hospital, which I know was nicer for her. But whereas Bethesda was walkable, with restaurants, parks, and shopping centers nearby, the VA in Richmond was more isolated. Even so, I was able to start doing more recreational activities, including going to a movie and then to a mall a few days later! Even though I was still a long way from driving myself, these little outings were part of my therapy as I learned how to navigate with a body that moved, felt, and looked very different from the one I was used to.

It was pretty obvious I was a combat-wounded vet, and every time I went out, people would stop me and want to talk. At first, I wasn't sure how to respond when people said, "Thank you for your service," but it felt least strange to just say, "You're welcome!" It wasn't quite what I wanted to convey, but it at least gave me a genuine reply I could offer with a smile. The outpouring of love and support from people was remarkable. Pearle Vision gave me a steep discount on my glasses and Ruth's Chris covered our meal when I sat down to my first steak in seven months. There was a part of me that felt a little uncomfortable accepting that kind of generosity, especially since I knew there were countless other veterans, whose injuries weren't as visible as mine, who could have used that kindness just as much. But I came to learn that people genuinely wanted to show honor and appreciation, and their gestures meant as much to them as they did to me. It was deeply humbling.

There were other surprising gestures of support as well. One that stands out involved an older nurse at Richmond who noticed my feet were in awful shape—a combination of injuries, blood-flow issues, and "deployment foot" from their being crammed into sweaty boots for months when I went without a shower. I used to joke that the nurse had a fetish, because she always seemed so excited to work on my feet—but she whipped them into shape! Whatever she did over those next few weeks almost completely healed me up and eliminated any pain I had been having in my feet. It's funny how someone can bring enthusiasm to a job you would never want to touch, and even if it's something small, can change your whole outlook. Walking was less painful, which meant I did it more, which meant interacting more and more with the world, which meant I was training my body and mind how to adapt to my new life. Which meant I was that much closer to reclaiming my life.

I still had to make the occasional trip up to Bethesda for specialized surgeries. We drove straight up I-95 past the National Museum of the Marine Corps, the peak of its roof reminiscent of the flag at Iwo Jima visible from the interstate; the stories of the incredible campaigns of Marines in the past and exhibits on Marine Corps Medal of Honor recipients were on exhibit inside. I liked catching a glimpse of the building every time we rolled past Quantico. It was a reminder that I was part of a long tradition, stretching back to 1775, instead of one wounded Marine, isolated from his unit.

Despite the continued surgeries, it was clear that I had moved into a new phase of recovery. I began to eat real food again, and practiced feeding myself with my left hand. By the middle of February, I was even able to stop speech therapy; my jaw and tongue had healed enough that I was able to speak normally.

Nick had been moved up to Boston for rehab, at his family's request. We got word that he was up walking and starting to talk, which was, of course, amazing to hear. Meanwhile, I reconnected with Stinson and his wife, Tesa, at the Richmond VA, and the three of us had so much fun together. I would say that we laughed until our sides hurt, but at the time I hurt pretty much all over and I imagine that Stinson did, too. Still, we found a way to have some good times in the hospital.

Tesa had found out she was pregnant just before we deployed and was getting nearer to her late-March due date now, and Stinson was in a wheelchair, of course, so I tried to be the one to shuffle down the hall to visit them instead of making them come to me. Stinson had a great sense of humor—you have to enjoy some gallows humor to keep yourself from getting overwhelmed when you're stuck in the hospital for so long. Once, when I walked in his door, he yelled, "Carpenter— heads up!" and tossed something at me. I managed to catch it with my left hand, and looked down to see that it was a grenade pepper shaker. Apparently, they'd gotten it as a wedding gift a few years before, and he'd asked his wife to bring it back with her the next time she returned from Pennsylvania, specifically to mess with me.

Revenge is a dish best served cold. Almost a year later, when Stinson and I were at Walter Reed together for treatment, Tesa and I stepped onto the elevator at the same time, and I pretended that the scary red-haired girl who had been hanging in the corner of my room during my hallucinations was on the elevator with us.

"What do you mean you don't see her?" I said, when Tesa insisted there was nothing there. "She's right next to you. Now she's staring at you!"

Then I got off on the very next floor, and let Tesa ride the rest of the way up wherever she was headed in an empty elevator, completely creeped out. She didn't find it quite as funny as I did ("I'm going to kill Kyle!" she told her husband), but Stinson thought it was hilarious.

Sometimes I did stuff I didn't intend to be funny but eventually realized must have seemed quirky to the people around me—then I totally ran with it. For example, my mouth felt dry quite a bit, so I used to burn through a lot of suckers just to keep it working. Once, as I was talking to Stinson, I reached into my sling, pulled out a Dum Dum, and popped it into my mouth.

"What the— Carpenter, where did that come from?" Stinson demanded.

"My sling," I told him, digging around for another flavor. "I always have five or six in here. You want one?"

"No!" he said, laughing hysterically. "Do you honestly carry around a stash of Dum Dum suckers in your sling?" I did, and I came to relish the looks on people's faces when I offered them one I had just pulled out of my bandages, like I was the world's weirdest magician.

During the almost three months I spent in hospitals I learned it is essential to find joy in whatever you can. Circumstances may be bad, but you are not your circumstances, and the way you choose to ride them out will set the tone for everything that follows.

My mom has always documented life's important milestones. Remember that filing system she keeps for my brothers and me? She turned that impulse up to an 11 while I was in the hospital, snapping photos of me and my medical staff nearly every day. My dad teased her about it. "Why are you taking pictures to remember the most difficult, terrible time of your life?" he would ask.

But Mom just brushed him off. "He's going to want these someday, to see how far he has come." And she was right. It's awe-inspiring for me to look back through those photos now. I know I will never be able to fully appreciate exactly how complicated and exacting all of those dozens of surgeries really were. Without the dedicated health-care providers who were fully invested in my recovery, I never would have survived, let alone been able to have an independent life outside of the hospital.

Even now, certain people are spoken of with special respect in my family—people like Dr. Turza, my trauma and skin-graft surgeon who had me over for dinner; Dr. Malone, the head trauma surgeon at Bethesda; Dr. Newman, who saved my arm; Dr. Foran, Dr. McDonald, Dr. Crecelius, and Dr. Auth, who did many of my facial and mouth surgeries; Dr. Nesti, who did my nerve-graft surgeries; Dr. Bachelor, who continued care on my arms after Dr. Newman left; all of the corpsmen and Army medics who sat in my dark room all of those nights just to monitor my vitals; and on and on. Those women and men, and countless others like them, are the real heroes of my story. We had no choice but to trust them, and they did not take that responsibility lightly. They had my life in their hands, and they worked to give it back to me as whole and hopeful as possible. They set me on a path to healing.

It's incredible how time heals, too. My brothers and I laugh about some of my hallucinations now, but at the time there was obviously nothing at all funny about them. But I was fortunate enough to only suffer temporary mental challenges; I am well aware that there are many combat-wounded veterans who have suffered TBI (traumatic brain injuries), often in addition to physical injuries, who will never be the same again. It's incredibly sobering to realize just how blessed I was that the damage I sustained was confined to my body. But of all the hallucinations, the one I can't seem to shake is the one about my funeral. I am still haunted by the feeling of emptiness and despair that I felt when I realized no one came. I think every day about how I am using the life that my health-care team worked so hard to preserve for me. Am I touching people's lives in a meaningful way? Am I leaving a legacy that matters? What am I doing with my second shot at life?

Chapter 10
It Starts at Home (Again)

FEBRUARY 2011

Early in the spring of 2011, my family was offered a surprising choice: I could stay at the VA hospital in Richmond, or I could go home to South Carolina to start physical therapy and wound care until the new barracks at Bethesda were completed in September.

The chance to recover in my own house, together with my family (and my dog!), instead of being stuck in a hospital five hundred miles away, seemed too good to be true. We understood that the arrangement was unconventional and would mean a tremendous amount of work and travel for my family to accommodate my extensive needs, but my medical team felt confident that my parents and brothers were up to the task. My mom volunteered to drive me to Bethesda whenever necessary if it meant we could all be together. I was approved to be released on convalescent leave.

I can't remember who made the joke—I think it was Price or Peyton—but we laughed that it was a good thing I never had any desire to go AWOL (not that I could have gotten very far!) because this would have been the perfect opportunity. I don't remember any of the six-hour drive from Richmond back home, but it was late February so I imagine the sky was gray and the scenery was pretty bleak. Even so, I don't think anything could have brought us down. Three months ago, my heart had seemed determined to flatline and there were serious doubts as to whether I would survive, let alone have a life outside of a hospital. Twelve weeks and twenty-four surgeries later, I was heading home, at least for a few months. For all the ups and downs since my injury, this was certainly one of the highest peaks.

After such a peaceful and uneventful drive, I was not prepared in any way for what awaited me as we turned into our neighborhood, led by the Patriot Guard Riders: What felt like hundreds of people were lined up, waving flags and holding signs that read WELCOME HOME KYLE! GOD BLESS OUR WOUNDED WARRIORS!

and TEAM KYLE. Price and Peyton were waiting to help me climb carefully out of our car and into our neighbor's golf cart, which was decked out in red, white, and blue. As we rolled down the street to our house, about a half mile away, people were cheering and celebrating like it was a Fourth of July parade. Cameras were flashing like crazy. As I recall, there were even police there, helping to mark the way. It was incredible—and also overwhelming.

For the past three months, other than occasional outings, my life had consisted of tiny hospital rooms that held no more than a few people. I passed folks in the hallway as I went for walks, but everyone was focused on their own rehab or their own patients. Even when I visited with friends, like Stinson and his wife, it was just us and the occasional nurse. Now, all of a sudden, I was being mobbed like a rock star and I wasn't ready for that. There were neighbors, high school friends I hadn't seen in three years, total strangers, newspaper reporters—and all their energy and excitement were directed at me. As we reached the end of my driveway, I climbed out of the golf cart and hugged my dad as a huge crowd enveloped us in what felt like a massive, citywide hug. I was simultaneously thankful, honored, humbled . . . and completely freaked out. I broke down on my dad's shoulder.

All of my senses, atrophied from months in a calm, sterile environment, were suddenly being bombarded with more love and encouragement than I knew what to do with. I wanted to celebrate with everyone, but I also wanted to escape. I wanted to let them know how much I appreciated what they were doing, but I also felt guilty for wanting to get away. I was shocked at my own emotional conflict: How could this much support and goodwill be so triggering? These were the people who had brought over casseroles to my family, watched the dog while they were in Bethesda, and spent countless hours on their knees for us. They had looked after my brothers when my parents needed to be with me, and they had looked after my parents when they needed the support. Why wasn't I more excited to see them all? Why didn't this feel like the greatest moment of my life? I had spent weeks hearing relief in people's voices that I was still "the same old Kyle," despite my injuries, but I was suddenly afraid that maybe I wasn't. I had convinced myself that my body was the only thing that needed rehabilitation, but what if that wasn't true? I had no idea how deeply normal all those emotions are for veterans in my shoes; all I knew was that I was flooded with fear. What if something had broken in me? What if I was never myself again?

My dad was eventually able to steer me into the house,

away from the loving crush of people in our yard. Once we were inside with the door shut, I started to calm down a little. The quiet sameness of everything—the same sofas, the same embarrassing photos on the wall from when we were little, the same knickknacks that help make a house feel like home—everything looked exactly as it had the previous July. It seemed strange that things could be exactly the same and yet changed so drastically. But mostly what mattered was that I would get to be home for the next six months and start learning how to live again in the real world. And one of those first lessons would clearly have to be how to engage with well-intentioned people.

Thankfully, inside the house, the only crush of energy I had to endure was from Sadie. As happy as everyone was to have me back, I think she was the most excited. Except to eat or take walks, Sadie never let me out of her sight. I had to sleep on the sofa because it was softer than my bed, and thus easier on my back and my arms. As well, although I'd slept on my back while in the hospital, the couch allowed me to kind of turn onto my side a little bit, which was a complete game-changer. Sadie slept in between my feet at the bottom of the couch (because she likes her space), but despite my constant moving around and even the occasional accidental kick as I tried to get comfortable, she never left—even though I couldn't pet her or rub her belly. I don't know how she knew I was so bad off, but she remained completely devoted to me, like my care and comfort were her personal responsibility.

Unfortunately, an attentive bichon frise couldn't solve every problem, and certain things turned out to be a bit more complicated than we'd hoped. Even then, however, the right people seemed to step in at the right time. On February 25, just a few days after we got home, I was admitted to the ER for hematemesis—put less elegantly, I was vomiting blood. When the nurse paged the attending physician, he described me as a "21-year-old male with a history of polytrauma." I'm not sure what Dr. Reedy was expecting when she approached my stretcher, but I'm pretty sure it wasn't someone who looked like me: right eye missing, a still-healing tracheostomy site, no teeth on the bottom jaw, shrapnel embedded just about everywhere, a black-lined face tattooed by the gunpowder that seared across it, and a right arm that was heavily bandaged and extremely fragile. I'll be honest; I wasn't expecting to see someone like Dr. Reedy, either. She has blond hair and is six-one flat-footed . . . and she was wearing heels that day. (Some of the old Vietnam veterans around the hospital affectionately called her their "Barbie doll.") She seemed to me like the tallest woman on the planet. Clearly, someone with her background and physical presence was used to being taken seriously. Even though my mom is five-two, I think they instantly recognized in one another a woman who could be a force of nature if she had to, and they respected that. I immediately felt the same wave of gratefulness for both of them.

The vomiting had stopped for the moment, so I smiled and introduced myself before we started reviewing my symptoms and history. We talked for a long time, and I could tell Dr. Reedy felt a personal commitment to my case; maybe it was just the extent of my injuries or maybe it was seeing the look of determination mingled with desperation on my mother's face. Whatever the reason, Dr. Reedy became a woman on a mission. She made an appointment for me to undergo an EGD (esophagogastroduodenoscopy) and I was diagnosed with "chronic gastritis due to prolonged stress." *You think?* I actually laughed. At least it all made sense. And she carefully studied all of my records—hundreds of pages just since November. Already I could tell that my team here was determined not to let me fail.

The primary care at the VA facility in Columbia and the physical and occupational therapy clinic at Lexington Medical Center would more than meet my needs, and they had outstanding doctors and therapists. Our biggest obstacle, though, was finding staff who were trained to treat injuries as extensive as mine; the military would pay for my care, but the system was so overwhelmed at the time that my family had to do the legwork of finding specialized providers in our area. After all, direct-hit grenade survivors are a rather limited bunch; there just aren't that many places that have the equipment and training in place to deal with this specific form of trauma. Proper wound care was my most pressing need, as infection still posed one of the greatest risks to my recovery. More than half of my body remained covered with fresh skin grafts and wounds in every stage of the healing process. My mom became an absolute machine, calling every medical facility near us, in increasingly larger circles. Everyone she spoke with had the same response: They would love to help but no one had the experience or facilities to handle the extensive washing and rebandaging I required every other day. Finally, her search reached the Augusta Burn Center, fifty miles away in Georgia. Although only a small percentage of my injuries were actual burns, the center had people who were trained in that degree of care and who were willing to work with me. Mom was so grateful she cried.

When we had a follow-up appointment at the VA two weeks later, Dr. Reedy admitted that she didn't understand how I was alive, let alone able to crack jokes. But humor was essential to my recovery; I've always been someone who cracks up at little things (sometimes at the most inappropriate times), and if I lost my sense of humor now, when I needed it most, how could I ever enjoy life again? Besides, she was right—I was alive against all odds. Sure, there was a lot of pain and frustration right now, but that was exactly why I was in a good mood: *I was alive, and we all recognized what a miracle that was.*

Speaking of the pain, I spoke to Dr. Reedy about my desire to get off as many medications—especially pain meds—as quickly as possible. At that point, I was on more than a dozen different prescriptions and I wanted to be done with them. She looked surprised and questioned me about my comfort. I admitted that I'd been better, but I had read too much about how easy it is for people to become addicted, even if they have no history of substance abuse and had no intention of overusing the medicines. That simply was not a road I wanted to test out, so I wanted to make sure I was off everything the second it was medically advisable. Also, as strange as this may sound, I wanted to make sure I was experiencing my injuries instead of just coasting through them. Pain is an important tool our body has for letting us know when something isn't right, and I didn't want my senses to be dulled as my body was trying to communicate with me, or as I was trying to communicate with the outside world. By that point, it was clear that some degree of pain was always going to be with me; I might as well learn how to live with it and figure out how to adjust as soon as possible. As I explained all this to Dr. Reedy, she gave me a strange look that she later told me was her way of saying, "Is this guy human?"

We had a similar thought about her. When it was time for us to leave, the pharmacy didn't have all my medications and wound care supplies ready, so they asked us to return later that day. Dr. Reedy must have read the exhaustion in my mom's face, because after we left she reached out to my mom and told her not to worry about it. Then she picked everything up after work and drove it to our home. *What doctor does that?*

When she arrived, I was asleep on the sofa, but I woke up to hear Dr. Reedy and my mom talking about my story. I offered to explain it more, so we all sat down and I laid out everything I remembered and everything I'd been filled in on later. We ended up looking at photos of the location and some of my official paperwork. In the middle of it all, Dr. Reedy suddenly looked over at me and asked, "Why did you join the Marines and take these risks?"

Part of me wanted to laugh and ask if my mom had put her up to asking that question, but instead I just told her simply: "To help fight bad people." She smiled and shook her head, and from that moment on she became my greatest advocate at the VA.

Right around that same time, I received word that I was to be honored by the South Carolina legislature, which humbled and amazed me. I was invited to be recognized on the floor of the state senate and to have a private meeting with then-Governor Nikki Haley. It was a moving recognition of not only my service, but the sacrifice of all the South Carolinians who were currently serving in support of Operation Enduring Freedom in Afghanistan.

The most memorable part of the day, however, was getting to finally meet Master Sergeant Williams, whose civilian job was as assistant-sergeant-at-arms for the South Carolina Senate—the same chaplain who had blessed me as I passed through Landstuhl on my way home in November. As he came out to meet my family in the parking garage when we arrived, I was overwhelmed with gratitude for this man and the prayer and attention he had offered me—and so many others just like me—at such a critical time. As quickly as severely injured patients are moved through Landstuhl, it was probably pretty rare that he was able to see one of "his" guys once they were in recovery. And it was probably pretty shocking for him to see someone who was so badly off just a few months ago up and walking around now.

MSG Williams gave me a big but gentle hug, since I knew he was mindful of my injuries. My mom gave him a massive bear hug when it was her turn; just knowing that there was someone from home who was looking out for their son during that time gave my parents immeasurable comfort. No one wants their hurting or dying child to be alone, and Chaplain Williams offered that presence that my family desperately wished they could.

Knowing that he would be at the ceremony that day, I wanted to give him a token of our gratitude. "Look at the inside cover," I said, handing MSG Williams a copy of a devotional book. The night before, I had spent about an hour trying to manipulate the pen in my left hand to write out what I wanted to tell him:

People meet in terrible, wonderful ways. I'm thankful we did.
With love, Kyle

Thank you. Believe in purpose.

Chaplain Williams had provided one of the most beautiful ministries possible: he was home for me when

I couldn't be at home. Funny how something you don't remember can also be something you will never forget.

My new routine involved physical or occupational therapy four days a week, with a drive to Augusta for wound care every two to three days. Every two to three weeks, Mom and I would drive five hundred miles up to Bethesda for another surgery or assessment. It was a grueling schedule for her, but she never once complained. Those eight-hour drives up I-95 were just like our daylong road trips from my childhood, where we would explore as far as we could drive and still make it back in time for dinner. Of course, surgery is always a bummer, but it was encouraging to see how pleased the D.C. team in Bethesda was with my progress. Now that they were no longer concerned with the basics, like making sure they could keep my heart rate stabilized or trying to save my remaining eye, we were able to focus on procedures that would allow me to work on more precise rehabilitation and adaptation. For example, I had total wrist drop from my radial nerve being severed; I couldn't lift my hand at all. As it was, I could only grasp an object by raising my hand above it and allowing my fingers to fall around the item, then tightening them. The hope was that I would eventually be able to retrain my body and brain to enable my wrist to bend to neutral so that I would have more control over my hand. Driving, writing, eating, and typing all drastically improve if you can at least lift your wrist to be level with your forearm, something most people take for granted.

I quickly came to love my health-care teams at home as much as I did my team at Bethesda. Julie Durnford was incredible. "Dr. Julie," as I called her, had tremendous patience and creativity as we tried all the different exercises and techniques possible to maximize my movement and flexibility. At first, a lot of our time was spent carefully working the muscles and joints of my hands to keep them pliable, since I wasn't able to move them myself. We joked that it is impossible to spend hours sitting across from someone, holding their hand, and not start spilling your deepest secrets. I told Dr. Julie she was my therapist in more ways than one. There was also a sweet old lady in her eighties who would often be seated next to me; she always pretended to make passes at me and called herself a "cougar." I loved the feeling of quiet community at the clinic, where I was greeted by name.

It may not sound like much, but that physical therapy was exhausting. I wasn't simply learning to do basic tasks again, like brushing my teeth or holding a fork—I was retraining my brain to work damaged muscle groups in new ways, or to engage completely different muscles than I had ever used for a task before. Everything was a physical and mental workout. I remember the first time I was able to flex my wrist; Dr. Julie and I had been working on it for weeks with no progress—no amount of concentration or willpower could force my wrist to move that way. Then one day, some random synapse from my brain fired in the right way, and my hand lifted up. I hadn't even been trying at the time, but my brain had been working behind the scenes to rebuild neural pathways, and suddenly, I could do it. Dr. Julie and I just about threw a ticker-tape parade. A few days later—and fully eight months after my injury—I managed to put on my socks by myself for the first time. It was a long and excruciating process—I think I struggled for ten minutes on each foot—but I just sat on the chair, sighed, and smiled when I finally did it. I was winning!

At the end of each therapy session, I would spend a half hour or so on a hand cycle or modified exercise bike that provided extended, low-impact joint manipulation. The machines were lined up along a large picture window that looked out over a strip mall and gas station, so the view wasn't exactly spectacular (at Naval Hospital Camp Pendleton, for example, the physical therapy bikes look out over the Pacific Ocean), but I loved those bikes all the same. There was something peaceful and centering about the smooth motion of moving my limbs without having to make a concentrated, deliberate effort to force my body to cooperate with my intentions. The feeling of being able to do something—anything—gracefully was also empowering. I knew I was reclaiming my body and my life, one tiny muscle twitch at a time.

After my initial panic at my welcome-home parade, I gradually came to be more and more comfortable with interacting with people, as well as dealing with surprises. Unquestionably, the best surprise was when Griffin Welch and Jared Lilly suddenly showed up at my house one Friday night in March, about two weeks after 2/9 returned from deployment. I stared at them for half a second in disbelief, then broke into the hugest smile as they walked in. I couldn't believe that those two guys were standing in the middle of my living room. They had already driven five hours up to see me in Richmond; now they'd driven five hours south to visit my parents' home? But this wasn't just a social call; they were there to help with my at-home wound care so that my mom could have a break. It was one of the most beautiful gestures of friendship I have ever witnessed. It's rare that I am speechless, but I was then.

That first time, it took them over an hour to figure out how to unwrap the wounds, properly wash them, and then reapply clean bandages in the right way and with the right amount of tension in the wrap. My mom patiently talked them through the whole process, and I couldn't help but think that I had been blessed with the greatest family, friends, and fellow Marines anyone could ever hope for. I was in the best mood for the next week, thinking about that visit. And then I was amazed again when they showed up the following weekend, too. Welch and Lilly would drive nearly ten hours round-trip from Camp Lejeune to South Carolina once a month for the next six months, which was pretty remarkable given that they were in the middle of their workup for their second deployment back to Marjah. In retrospect, given everything they were doing for us, I probably should *not* have let out a scream sometime around the third or fourth visit when they were rewrapping my wounds. They both dropped the bandages with a horrified look. I actually think Welch's heart might have stopped. I could not hold it together. I started hysterically laughing and told them I was just messing with them. It was probably kind of mean on my part, but the looks on their faces were priceless, and I was counting on them not wanting to punch a guy who had just cuddled a grenade.

In June 2011, I had one of the most difficult medical visits of my time at home. Two weeks earlier I had undergone a surgery at Bethesda (I think this one was around my thirtieth) on my left forearm to try to identify nerves that still functioned and surgery on my right arm to harvest nerves to transplant elsewhere, as well as surgery to make some repairs, including removing scar tissue from some tendons in my elbow. The surgeons also removed some of the hardware that had previously been inserted to help hold the bones in my right arm together.

Something hadn't gone right with the healing, though, and I ended up with an infection at the surgery sites. Dr. Reedy had to remove twenty-one sutures as well as treat the infection, and the pain was excruciating—some of the worst I'd had in months. But I didn't want to give in to the hurt or allow it any power or control over me, because I didn't want that to open the door to make excuses or slide backward in my recovery, especially since I had been making such encouraging progress. When Dr. Reedy kept asking me to describe the nerve pain and I didn't say much, she kept pressing me. Finally I admitted that I had a horrible sensation in my left palm whenever anything touched it, but that it did feel better when I immersed my hand in water.

"Is there anything else?" she asked.

"Oh, if I didn't have this I'd be perfect," I replied. I could tell she wasn't sure if I was being relentlessly positive or an absolute smart-ass. To be fair, it was probably a bit of both.

By August, I was down to only four prescriptions, including just one pain pill at bedtime so I could sleep. That accomplishment, combined with my new, custom prosthetic right eye, had me almost bouncing off the walls with excitement because I had reached a point in my recovery where I could begin driver rehabilitation training, which was one step closer to independence. Not long afterward, however, I started having episodes of dizziness. Dr. Reedy demanded I come in immediately, because she was concerned the patch that had been placed in an effort to repair the hole caused by shrapnel that had penetrated my neck and carotid artery might be failing or it might be causing a blockage that could lead to a stroke. Thankfully, everything looked fine and I was just ordered to take it easy for a few weeks, to let my body catch up with all of the progress that was happening at such an incredible speed.

And "incredible" is right—the rate of progress I had made from being clinically dead due to a grenade blast to learning to drive again on my own in less than nine months was almost unimaginable. Even looking back on it now, I am in awe of everything that happened in that first year after the blast. Yes, my stubbornness, tenacity, and competition with myself certainly played a role in it, but what it really comes down to is the untiring dedication of the people who rallied around me, from my family and friends to my health-care team and community. I will never know just how much they all did—much of it behind the scenes—to get me the support, resources, equipment, facilities, and permissions to accomplish everything I was able to. Never have I appreciated more the expression "It takes a village." The military took a risk releasing me to home care for those six months, but it paid off beautifully. No one ever acted as if my care was a burden; in fact, everyone treated me as if each task was a celebration of the fact that I'd been given a second chance. Admittedly, it was a little uncomfortable at first; my parents had always raised us to be humble, not demand the spotlight, and to try to put others first. And now, my concerns and my needs and my comfort and my goals all seemed to be front and center.

But no one ever made me feel guilty about that. My parents never complained about the endless appointments and days on the road. My brothers could have resented the fact that I was occupying so much of Mom and Dad's emotional energy, but they never once said or did anything that indicated they felt that way. The health-care facilities that took over my care could have viewed me as a burden to their system and a drain on resources, but every single staff member, from doctors to nurses to orderlies, and even fellow patients, treated me as if my recovery were their first and only priority. Church members acted like it was their honor to have my recovery dominate the prayer request list. Everywhere I turned, it seemed people were invested in *me*—and I learned to accept the help and support that was being offered so willingly and selflessly. I know caretakers are the unsung heroes of any serious medical situation—the people who do the day-in-and-day-out tasks of keeping someone comfortable, taking them to the bathroom, remembering their pill schedule, accommodating their diet, helping them get dressed, keeping them company, cheering them up, celebrating their good days, walking them through their bad days . . . I can't imagine how exhausting it must be to suddenly find yourself in a full-time, around-the-clock job of taking care of someone else. And yet this was the role that various people took on for me. It was this strength and support when I was still at my most broken, physically, that enabled me to begin to rebuild a normal life.

I knew from Bethesda and Richmond that I could function just fine in the hospital—but that wasn't real life. When the environment is strictly controlled and there's always a nurse available within ten seconds if someone presses the call button, everything becomes deceptively simple. Don't get me wrong—it was exactly where I needed to be in those critical weeks immediately following my injuries. But I also needed an opportunity to dip a toe back into the real world. I needed to know that there was life on the other side of the hospital. I needed to be reminded that the world had still carried on despite my injuries. Ultimately, it was up to me to decide whether I was going to fight back through rehab in the hopes of one day reclaiming an independent life, or if I would decide it was all too overwhelming to try. Would I catch up or give up?

The support, physical care, and therapeutic training I received at home as I started over again formed the bedrock for every other challenge that was to come. Although there was still a lifetime of surgeries and rehab in my future, physically, I was light-years ahead of where any of us could have dared hope.

The emotional side of things, however, was a different story.

Chapter 11
The Past Truly Is the Past

APRIL 2011

I wasn't just physically exhausted, I was emotionally drained.

From the moment I regained consciousness back in December, I had been putting on a strong face for my family. I thought if I could reassure them I was okay, it would be easier for them to deal with what happened to me. I am a Marine, which means the instinct to protect others is second nature, and that instinct was working overtime now.

At first, there was too much going on for me to get down. My surgeries were only a few days apart, and there were always people in my room coming to visit or something happening to keep my interest. As well, I was out of it a lot of the time during the first few months. But the more I came back to myself, the more pressure I started to feel to be strong emotionally for everyone around me. It wasn't pressure from my family by any means, but my mom's eyes looked terrified as she tried to reassure me as I was coming out of my hallucinations, and my dad had a catch in his throat whenever we talked about my pain. I hated the worry and stress I was causing them. I knew if I was okay, they would be okay, and I clung to that as I pushed through those first few grueling months of surgeries and beginning rehab.

I knew every member of my support team was worn down emotionally, struggling to help me find my new normal—struggling to help our family find our new normal. It was more than the endless hospital trips and surgeries and skin grafts and adaptive exercises; it was getting used to the constant pain and the feeling of the shrapnel still trapped in my body. From what I could see with my remaining eye, the world looked very much the same. My mom and dad looked exactly like they had before I'd shipped out. My brothers were taller but otherwise the same boys I'd always known. But I knew that what they saw was forever changed. Every time they looked at me they couldn't help but see my wounds.

I had been the one to enlist, but now my family was serving alongside me.

The problem was that there was no getting away from my injuries. Even though I was back at home, there was no pretending that life was normal or would ever be the same again. There wasn't a way to escape what had happened. I was going to be living in a seriously injured body for the rest of my life, and we all knew it. Every jolt of pain, every basic task I couldn't perform, was a reminder that life as I knew it was over. I could never escape that one moment on a rooftop halfway around the world. As tough as I wanted to be—as I was trying to be—I couldn't hold on much longer.

I was sitting at the kitchen counter, carefully trying to balance the spoon in my left hand—one of many basic skills I was having to relearn—and attempting to eat a bowl of cereal, which wasn't easy given that my maxillofacial surgeries were not yet complete, so what remained of my jaw and teeth was still basically useless. Struggling to hold on to my spoon, milk and cereal dribbling down my chin, I suddenly felt something inside me break. Every emotion, every fear, every effort to be brave to protect my family from my pain, came pouring out faster than the cereal I couldn't chew.

It was 10:00 P.M. after another exhausting day of physical therapy and wound care. I just wanted a bowl of cereal—something basic and comforting. Something from my old life. I retrieved the box and the milk and carefully began to pour, a major accomplishment. I laughed a little as I looked at the box in my hand: Wheaties. I don't remember who was on the box, but I do remember thinking how funny it was that fixing myself "the breakfast of champions" felt like such a major victory.

For a few seconds, I was a normal guy, pouring himself a bowl of Wheaties. It was nice. It was better than nice. I had managed to do something entirely on my own! I wasn't completely helpless. I felt strong, empowered, and hopeful. For a moment, I had almost forgotten I was injured. I raised the spoon to my mouth to take that first bite . . . and then reality came flooding back: I couldn't chew. I didn't have the luxury of forgetting. My injuries wouldn't let me.

The sound of my mom walking into the kitchen hadn't even registered. Maybe I was too upset to pay attention, but it was probably due to the fact that my hearing was still too impaired to detect subtle sounds. She had peeked in just to say hello, but when she saw me slumped over the counter with my shoulders heaving, she clicked into "mom mode." I think it was the first time she had seen me show any raw emotion since I had come out of my coma, and she immediately knew something was deeply wrong. She ran across the room and gently but firmly wrapped her arms around me. "Are you in pain?" she asked.

Through sobs, I managed to choke out one devastating question: "Look at me. Who is ever going to love me again?"

There was a moment of silence. I pulled my head up and stared at her face, where I could see that my words absolutely tore her heart in two, and I immediately regretted saying them. But my mom responded the only way a mother can: She hugged me again. "I promise you are going to get through this and things are going to get better," she said, her face pressed into my shoulder. "Someday, someone is going to love you and you are going to be happy for the rest of your life. I promise."

As we sat together in the kitchen, with the overhead lights reflecting back against the darkness outside, I had a realization: I could spend my life sitting at that counter, or I could get up and live.

I chose to get up and live.

That spring night, five months after the grenade attack, everything changed for me. As I sat and cried with my mother, I resolved that I was going to move forward and create a new life out of what I had been handed. My mom stayed strong while I lost it, which lifted from my shoulders that self-imposed pressure to never show a crack in optimism or resolve. It may have been the relief of seeing that role reversal that let me know I could be honest about my pain and my fears, or it could have just been the Wheaties living up to their promise. Whatever the case, I suddenly felt a shift.

I was going to let go of all pretense and any roles I felt I had to play. I didn't have to pretend to be strong if I didn't feel that way. I didn't have to act like nothing bothered me. Truthfulness had always been emphasized in my home and now, I realized that I could move forward boldly and honestly, allowing my family to help me, to feel with me, to cry with me, and to celebrate with me. As long as I kept pretending that everything was fine, I was never going to be able to move beyond what had happened because I would never allow my present life to be what it actually was. I thought I was being strong, but all I was really doing was clinging to the past.

That moment at the kitchen counter was raw. My vow wasn't backed by deep, reasoned thinking. I just knew that I was at a crossroads. I could choose to move forward or I could choose to stay put, but only one of those options was going to count for anything. If I stayed locked in the vision of myself as a broken, shattered, incomplete person, that was all I would ever allow myself to be. That one bit of insight was one of the most important steps I took in my entire recovery process. In the months and years that followed, I would look back on that incident at the kitchen counter as the moment that changed everything—my outlook, my attitude, my trajectory for the future.

For weeks afterward, I would wake up wondering, *Now what?* Every morning started with a question for which I didn't have an answer, except to do whatever the next thing was that day. I developed a daily mantra, and I still say something similar to myself each morning: "I don't know what I want to do or how I'm going to do it or where I might end up, but as long as I work hard, try to do the right thing, try to be a good person, and try to help people—I can't go wrong doing that."

I realize that is not the most profound piece of wisdom ever uttered, but in those early days it kept me focused on what was ahead, which in turn laid the groundwork for all that I accomplished afterward. My approach to everything changed. Suddenly, occupational therapy wasn't about recovering the motor skills I had lost, it was about challenging myself to see what abilities I could master. Physical therapy wasn't about regaining movement I no longer had, it was about seeing how hard I could push myself to make my arms and legs do what I wanted them to. By leaving the past in the past, I allowed my future to take shape.

The more I fought *for* my future instead of *against* my past, the more I realized that there wasn't just life for me on the other side of this—there was life for me in the middle of it. My life wasn't going to start again after my recovery, because, truthfully, my recovery is not something that will ever be complete or ever be over. But by letting go of a world where I wasn't injured, I could focus on the life I *had* been given—a second chance that not everyone is lucky enough to get.

Just a few weeks later, there was a knock on the front door and a FedEx man with three large metal containers to drop off. There they were, all my personal effects: my uniforms, my gear, the stuff I had packed to go on deployment with me, the letters I had received in Afghanistan. Exactly where they had been hanging out for the past six months was a mystery, but they were back in South Carolina now—"Past Kyle" time capsules sitting in our front yard, still coated with mud and dust from Afghanistan. There was the scrapbook my mom had put together for me before I left, a couple of random CDs, my note-taking book, a pair of gloves an Irish soldier had given me on deployment, my Bible, and a paperback Harry Potter book. There was even a copy of one of my favorite books, *The Giver* by Lois Lowry, stamped with the words "King Academy" in the front. I must have checked it out from the library at school and never returned it. (Sorry, King Academy!)

As I dug through those boxes, I remembered a thousand things I didn't realize I had forgotten. It was like traveling back in time to before the grenade and before the deployment and catching a glimpse of who I was just a few months before both. As thrilled as I was to see all that stuff again, it was also difficult to think about what had changed since I'd first loaded those boxes. But as I walked back into the house to grab a glass of water, I saw *the* stool—second from the left at the kitchen counter—and I remembered the resolution I had made not to dwell on what couldn't be changed.

That shipment brought me nostalgia but not regret. It reminded me of what I had felt called to do and how I had acted on it, and the sense of pride and fulfillment that gave me. Now I was creating a new life out of that by letting go of my old ideas about what life should look like. That gave me a sense of pride, too. And it was especially important for me in the coming months, as I prepared to return to D.C. for treatment.

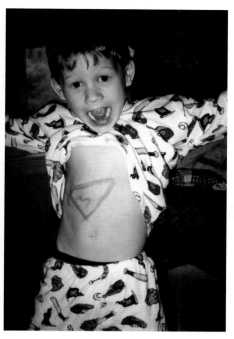

Learning to salute early!
Me at age three.

The Superman logo my dad would draw
on my chest with a Sharpie

Teammate John Gardner and I after competing in the SCISA (South Carolina
Independent School Association) North South All Star Game

In front of the famous silver "hatches" on Parris Island, following boot camp graduation. The only people to ever walk through these doors are Marine Corps recruits. They are a symbolic threshold between the outside world and Parris Island. Above them reads: "Through these portals pass prospects for America's finest fighting force."

School of Infantry graduation, Camp Geiger, NC. With me are
Mike Tinari (*left*) and Scott Condrey (*right*).

3rd Platoon, Fox Company, 2nd Battalion, 9th Marines

Patrol Base Beatley, Marjah, Helmand Province. Our home away from home.

An MH-53 Super Stallion helicopter delivers a supply drop bringing us food, water, ammunition, and medical supplies.

Children headed to the field for work outside the walls of our patrol base

Hanging out with our interpreter, Buck (*middle*), and an Afghan National Army soldier (*left*) during downtime in between patrols

On foot patrol within our area of operation

Posing with Shady, who reminded me fondly of my dog, Sadie, back at home

Utilizing an elevated rooftop position to provide "overwatch" protection for fellow squad member movement on the ground

Me with fellow Marine and best friend, Nick Eufrazio,
patrolling together as we did every day

Yes, even Marines take selfies. I had gone up to visit Nick on post.

Even nine years later, if you go to Google Earth, you can still see the hole in the roof caused by the grenade that changed my life forever. *Image courtesy of Google Maps.*

What was left of the M4 rifle I was holding at the time of the blast

A reunion with the Air Force medevac crew, call sign "Pedro," nine years after they picked me up off the battlefield and saved my life

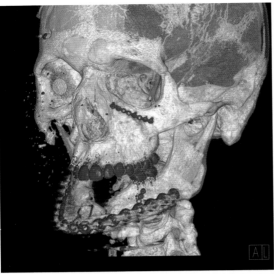

A 3-D facial reconstruction of a CAT scan. Taken at Walter Reed on March 20, 2012.

An X-ray of my right humerus before the thirteen-hour surgery to repair the fractures

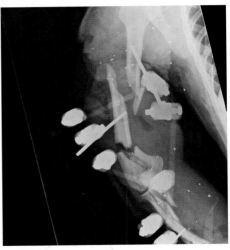

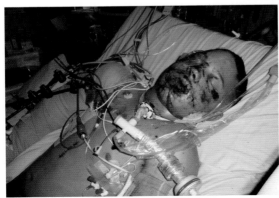

In the ICU at Landstuhl in Germany. By the time this photo was taken, I had already been resuscitated twice.

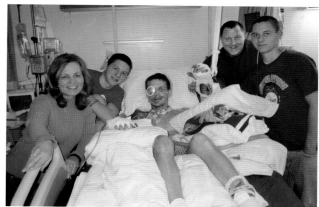

At Walter Reed with my family, who has never left my side

Commandant of the Marine Corps General James F. Amos, left, and Sergeant Major of the Marine Corps Carlton W. Kent, right, conducted my Purple Heart award ceremony in my room at Walter Reed.

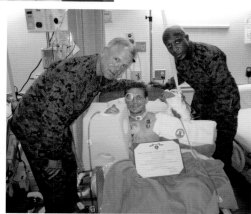

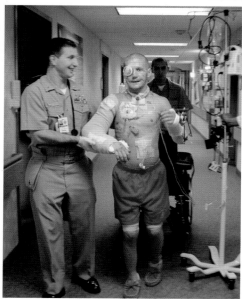

My first victory lap around the fifth floor. The smallest of steps eventually completes the grandest of journeys.

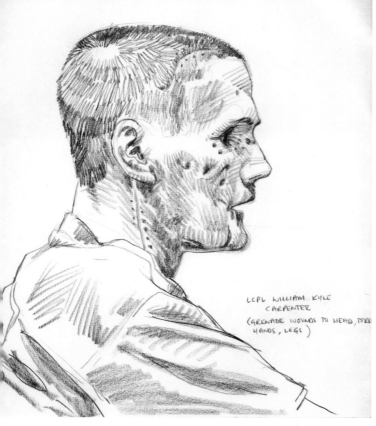

LCPL WILLIAM KYLE
CARPENTER
(GRENADE WOUNDS TO HEAD, EYES
HANDS, LEGS)

A sketch done of me in the VA hospital in Richmond, Virginia. Marine Corps Chief Warrant Officer Mike Fay, a combat sketch artist, drew this for a project that ran in the *New York Times*.

My team of doctors at the VA hospital in Richmond

Army Major Dr. Lauren Turza, one of my lead trauma surgeons at Walter Reed, has become a great friend. We grew so close that she named her first son after me!

With Dr. Debra Reedy, my doctor at the VA hospital who took care of me while I was recovering at home before returning to Walter Reed. This picture was taken after my graduation from the University of South Carolina.

Air Force Colonel Dr. Debra Malone, my other lead trauma surgeon, after we delivered a speech together in Hershey, PA

With my friend Chuck Williams, the chaplain who prayed over me in Germany

With Ryan Craig and his mother, Jennifer Miller. Jennifer held our hands on the flight from Ramstein Air Base, Germany, until we landed in the United States.

A proud moment for all Marines

Walking along the Rose Garden at the White House. The president was asking me about school and life. *Official White House Photo by Pete Souza.*

In the Blue Room with the President, the First Lady, and my medical team just after my ceremony

Mom offering me her shoulder, as she always has

Celebrating mile seventeen of my third Marine Corps Marathon

Flanked by fellow wounded warriors and Army Rangers in a helicopter during our trip back to Afghanistan in 2015 to visit troops, the U.S. embassy, and the hospitals that saved us

Skydiving over Dubai before speaking at the U.S. embassy in 2017

Thankful for the opportunity to keep my promise to myself and my parents. Graduation Day 2017. Go Gamecocks!

Honored to have been the "Keep Pounding" drummer for the Carolina Panthers

Life is beautiful. At the Smithsonian Institution's National Portrait Gallery, which inducted the photograph of me that appears on this cover of this book (by Mike McGregor) into its collection.

SEPTEMBER 15, 2011

Two major Washington-area military medical centers, the naval hospital at Bethesda and Walter Reed Army Hospital, were combined in 2011. The new Walter Reed National Military Medical Center in Bethesda was christened on September 15, and had greatly expanded barracks on-site that could now house combat veterans in need of longer-term treatment. Guys like me. I actually got to cut the ribbon at the groundbreaking with Secretary of Defense Leon Panetta. I could barely hold the scissors, but it was surreal to be part of the rebirth of the hospital that had once saved my life.

For the past six months, I had been living at home and receiving treatment locally in between surgery trips to Bethesda. Now that Walter Reed had expanded its capacity to allow for more full-time patients, I was returning to stay at the hospital full-time. The care I received in Lexington and Augusta had been phenomenal, and I hated to leave behind the health-care teams I had there, but I also had to be realistic about what my wounds required in terms of ongoing, specialized care. A grenade explosion isn't exactly an everyday sort of injury, and a major military medical facility was going to be better equipped for treating its aftermath.

It was great to be back around other Marines at Walter Reed; the energy and camaraderie were healing. There were people in every stage of recovery—guys fresh from Afghanistan and Iraq, and guys who had been in treatment longer than I had. Together, we were able to remind each other that we were still Marines, no matter how severely we were wounded or how long we had been in the hospital.

The Wounded Warrior Battalion (WWB) became a huge factor in my healing process at Walter Reed. Initially, it was a program run by Marine Corps reservists designed to help injured and ill Marines with some basic administrative work while they were being treated during extended hospital stays. When the surge began in 2010 and military hospitals began to be inundated with combat-wounded Marines, General James F. Amos, Commandant of the Marine Corps, revamped the program by staffing it with active-duty Marines. The goal was to help patients maintain their identity as Marines while they were separated from their units for treatment. Wounded Warrior Battalion West operated from Camp Pendleton, California, and Wounded Warrior Battalion East operated from Camp Lejeune, North Carolina, but both battalions had detachments at various facilities around the country. They assisted us in managing our appointments, mentoring each other through our treatments and recovery, providing morale-boosting activities, and even making sure we got our weekly haircuts to stay within Marine Corps regulations. They also helped our families connect with support and resources. As I settled into my new life at Walter Reed, WWB helped me see that letting go of the past didn't mean letting go of my identity: I was still myself, still a Marine, and still a young guy who could have fun and enjoy life. I was in no way denying what had happened to me or pretending that my injuries never happened, but I was able to go forward with my life with room for my new reality without making it central to my identity. My past shaped me, but it did not control me.

At some point, everyone will face a rock-bottom moment when the past looms too large to overcome and a hopeful future seems too far out to imagine. It's difficult to prepare yourself for that moment because it's impossible to know what will trigger it. It might be a major setback that knocks you to the ground, or it could be something so seemingly minor and innocuous as trying to eat a bowl of cereal. The point is, you can't really do much ahead of time to prevent that moment from happening; you may not even be able to brace yourself for the impact. All you can do is commit yourself to surviving for another day by recognizing that you can't change what is behind you—only what lies ahead.

You may even wonder if it is possible to move on—and it might not be without professional guidance to help you process everything that your past represents. It's not a process that can be rushed; you have to be honest with yourself as to whether or not it is time to let go of the past. Maybe the answer is "not yet," and that's okay, but at some point, you have to be willing to say, "From this day forward, I am choosing to live." Too often, we fall into the trap of thinking we need to have everything figured out before we can act. You don't have to have a road map before you set out; you don't even have to know the direction you're traveling. You just have to be willing to move and leave the past behind.

The unfortunate part is that those emotions of hopelessness and doubt may resurface again and again as you push ahead. But if you can focus on the moment when you said, "This is it. I've made my decision," you may find it is a little bit easier to recommit yourself to the path. Don't be discouraged when it feels like you are moving backward. I know: That's easy to say and difficult to do. But it is an essential part of healing. Letting the past stay in the past means that you recognize that any setbacks moving forward are simply part of your new journey, not a sign of failure.

That choice, that resolution simply to get up off that stool in the kitchen, was the most significant choice I could have made. Because it *was* a choice. It was when I resolved not to be controlled by the worst moment of my life. If I had given in, I'd essentially have been handing my future over to the enemy who threw that grenade on the roof, and he had already taken enough from me. My life, and my future, belong only to me, and I made the decision that I was worth fighting for.

Chapter 12
Jump

WALTER REED
September 2011

Staff Sergeant Paul Ramirez was passing through Warrior Cafe in Building 62 at Walter Reed, when he spotted a bald, heavily scarred, skinny young man in a green polo shirt and an older man who looked like he might be his father. They both seemed a bit lost.

Staff Sergeant Ramirez had been detached earlier that year from his duty station as an instructor at MATSS-1, a Marine Corps training school at Naval Air Station Meridian, Mississippi, to help build up the Marine Wounded Warrior Regiment (WWR) at the newly combined and expanded Bethesda/Walter Reed medical center. The goal of WWR was to help service members who were struggling to keep track of their appointments and checkups, surgeries, and follow-ups. These military men and women were trying to recover while continuing their service, in whatever limited capacity they could. For many long-term patients at Walter Reed—whether combat-wounded, seriously injured in off-duty accidents, or facing inpatient care for a condition like cancer—it was easy to lose their identity as active-duty service members when they were separated so long from the rest of the military. Administrators, which we referred to as "section leaders," like Staff Sergeant Ramirez were there to help ill and injured Marines navigate the system but also to connect them with resources that would motivate them to be Marines again, and to help them reclaim a part of their identity that may have felt like it was erased.

That is why, as soon as he recognized that the young man and his father needed help, Staff Sergeant Ramirez walked over and asked if he could answer any questions. And that was how I first met Paul; at the time, however, I just knew he was someone I had to call "Staff Sergeant Ramirez." A day or two later, when I got my WWR assignment, I was placed under his supervision. Since I and others at Walter Reed were still active-duty Marines but unable to operate with our units to which we'd been assigned or in our same job capacity, the Wounded Warrior Regiments became our new units and the hospitals our new duty stations. Our new "job" was to heal. WWR quickly proved to be one of the most important aspects of my recovery, and my mentorship with Paul became one of the most important friendships of my life.

Because I now had a Marine unit, I was moved to a building on the Walter Reed base that didn't allow my family to stay with me as they had in the hospital. It was difficult to say goodbye to my parents, but I was also excited for the next chapter of my life to start. The first year after the injury had been a nonstop cycle of surgery, recovery, physical therapy, surgery, recovery, physical therapy, surgery . . . I was still facing a cycle of surgeries and recovery, but now I was going through it with more physical independence and in a place where I would be reconnected with other wounded warriors and feel like a Marine again.

That group of Marines challenged, encouraged, and held one another accountable. It is one thing to have a doctor or a physical therapist tell you that you need to keep pushing; it's another thing to see a quadruple amputee, with a smile on his face, doing physical therapy every day. The Marines who had been in the regiment longer acted as mentors for the newer guys, refusing to treat them like broken toys or allow them to feel sorry for themselves.

It was early in my recovery when I learned one of the most important lessons of my life: Jump.

The vast majority of service members injured in combat are in their twenties and thirties—in other words, people who are young and were presumably healthy prior to the incident that landed them in the hospital. For many of them, their bodies had never failed them in any drastic or lasting way before; their physical capabilities had probably been an important part of their identity, whether as a service member, an athlete, or simply as an active, mobile individual. What's more, because of their age, many combat-injured service members are daunted by the possibility of being limited for the rest of their lives, which might be another forty, fifty, or sixty years. Would their bodies always hurt this much? Would their family have to move into a handicap-accessible house? Would they require full-time care? What kind of jobs would they be able to do? How would their injuries impact their marriage or their family? If they didn't yet have either, would anyone be willing to take on their new injuries in a relationship? Would children even be part of their future? In other words, the pain and feelings of constraint, restriction, inconvenience, and even worthlessness that might be dominating a person's life at that moment can often loom large as they try to imagine what kind of a future they have to look forward to.

I want to be very clear that I mean no disrespect toward the differently abled community and the people who were born that way or found their bodies permanently changed through noncombat means. I can only speak to what I have experienced and observed among my peers, and these emotions are common as wounded warriors struggle to adjust to a new reality that can seem overwhelming at first. For many, successful completion of occupational therapy seems so far down the road that it's hard to imagine life on the other side. For others, rehab is never going to restore their lives to anything close to what they once were, and this can easily lead to feelings of hopelessness. Most combat-wounded veterans have had limited exposure to differently abled communities prior to their injuries and are not aware of the unique culture of activities, support, and opportunities that exists these days for amputees, people in wheelchairs, people with spinal cord injuries, burn victims, and people living with the lasting effects of traumatic brain injuries. This is an area that has grown exponentially over the past twenty years, both in terms of available resources for adaptive activities and technology, and the changes are exciting. But that is little consolation to someone who is living in the hospital for the foreseeable future, facing months or years of continued surgeries and painful physical therapy.

These feelings of despair almost universally give way to some form of depression, often severe. Counseling can be a hugely important part of overcoming depression, but it's not always enough. Sometimes, the best thing to jump-start healing is to try to shatter every "norm." By forcing your body—your wounded, broken body—to do something extreme that you would never have considered before your injury, you are redefining what is possible for yourself and reestablishing the boundaries of what you can and can't do. It's not a matter of "snapping out of it" so much as it is a shock to the system. To remind yourself of the courage and life you still possess, you jump.

There are several wonderful people and groups that work in this area, and I was fortunate enough to connect with an inspirational fellow wounded warrior, Jason "Jay" Redman, who has founded a program called Jumping for a Purpose. A former Navy SEAL, Redman was shot multiple times, including in his face, so he understands firsthand what it is like to struggle with life-altering injuries, and he speaks to each group of wounded warriors before the aptly named "empowerment events" Jumping for a Purpose sponsors. Its mission is "to inspire combat-wounded warriors to overcome, by mitigating the effects of trauma, expanding personal capabilities, and inspiring our heroes to find individual and unique purpose to create the life they desire." As fundamental as those ideas may seem, their cultivation among combat-wounded veterans is extremely important.

Jumping for a Purpose is built around the idea that you have to force yourself back into life or you will find yourself focusing on what you can't do. By pushing yourself past your *pre*-injury comfort zone, you can come to terms with your real strength and resilience *post*-injury. The program has now been expanded to include Gold Star families who have lost a loved one in service, too, to help them find life after loss. And one way Jay and his team do this is by (in their words) "throw[ing] banged up people out of perfectly good airplanes." In other words, they take people skydiving.

At that time at Walter Reed, Jumping for a Purpose was one of the most anticipated aspects of recovery; guys were eager to sign up to participate while at the same time terrified of getting approved to do so. I wasn't sure my doctors were going to sign off on all my forms, but they did. In fact, I found out later that unless you are fresh out of surgery or have a condition that could be worsened by the adrenaline or sudden aggressive movements that accompany skydiving, they usually approve you to jump because it's good at reviving spirits and changing outlook. I was amazed and excited when I got the go-ahead from my medical team.

There was just one tiny problem: I am terrified of heights.

But I was not going to miss out on this opportunity; I had a nagging feeling that this was something I needed to do. So on a crisp fall day, my group took a bus about an hour away to an open field in rural Virginia. Once we arrived, I couldn't help but ask: *I don't really need to jump out of an airplane to feel alive, do I?* Apparently, I did.

"The only limitations you have are the ones you place on yourself," Jay told us. After a remark like that, there was no way I could back out.

We were instructed on the procedure and the safety measures, and we did some practicing while we were still safely on the ground. The next thing I knew, we were on a plane climbing almost straight up into the clouds. As we got impossibly high up and (I assumed) near our mark, I made the mistake of asking how much longer until our jump. The answer to the question I wish I'd never asked? "We're about halfway." Wonderful.

I was seated next to a triple amputee—Tyler Southern, an absolute wild man who only had a few fingers left on his remaining arm but who was 100 percent determined that he was bigger than his injuries. Watching him get psyched for the jump and then leap out of the plane with what was left of his body showed me that if he could do it, I could do it. We also had another triple amputee up there with us named Todd Love. Since his injuries, Todd had become certified as a parachutist and a diver, completed multiple Spartan Races using only his arms, and even wrestled an alligator. I mean, I was in the air with guys who were superhuman. If they could do all of that, surely I could muster the courage to step out of the airplane.

I gritted my teeth, closed my eyes, held my breath, and—jumped. We were all strapped to a professional jumper; in my case, it was a supercool dude and Red Bull athlete named Jeff Provenzano. Jeff helped steer us and man the equipment so that I could focus on the experience of the jump itself. And what an experience it was.

Weightlessness and recklessness. The two feelings swirled together as I plummeted toward the earth, screaming and laughing and grinning the entire way. The physical experience of soaring through the air is unbelievable, but every bit as amazing is the sense that *you are doing something insane, completely irresponsible, and perfectly epic.* For more than a year, I had been living in the safe confines of hospitals or under the protective, watchful care of my family. Every movement was slow and careful; every bump or stumble was cause for worry; everything was centered on my safety. Without realizing it, I had started to believe that I was made of glass. Even as I pushed myself to grow stronger or master a skill, there was a voice in the back of my head saying, "Be careful—your body isn't what it used to be." But now, as the ground got terrifyingly close, there was a sense of freedom—as if all those beliefs about being fragile or needing to play it safe melted away as I fell from thirteen thousand feet.

Forcing myself to jump, despite my terror, was another turning point in my recovery. I was fortunate enough to have emerged from my injuries with as few physical and emotional challenges as I did. And I had already had some breakthroughs, like my epiphany at the kitchen counter the previous April—but that didn't mean that I didn't still struggle. Sometimes epically. That's just the reality of dealing with the aftermath of a devastating injury or life circumstance. After that day, however, I knew that Jay Redman was right: My only limitations were the ones I put on myself. And as far as I was concerned, I wasn't going to set any more.

It is incredible to think about the places freedom can take you.

Freedom from self-imposed limits, combined with the lessons I'd learned about finding the joy during my last extended hospital stay, led me to try to find ways to not only cultivate my own enthusiasm, but to also share that with other people. Part of becoming "okay" again, whatever that means to someone, is how we choose to interact with the people around us. For me, one of the most rewarding ways I found was what my mom and I called the Dollar Bill Game.

I don't even recall how we came up with it, but on one of her visits to Walter Reed, we started placing random dollar bills in elevators for people to find. That was it—nothing much. I mean, does a single dollar make a huge difference to anyone at Walter Reed? Probably not. But the act of finding it can lift someone's spirits and make them think that maybe things are going to go their way that day. All told, the Dollar Bill Game probably cost us less than $30 over the length of my stay in the hospital, but it made me smile to think about someone's reaction when they discovered the dollar on the floor. Nobody knew it was us, so the favor couldn't be returned, and that was part of the joy. There is something powerful about feeling as if you have enough resources—emotional as well as financial—to share. For me, it felt like I had healed enough to be able to turn my focus outward instead of inward.

About two months after I arrived at Walter Reed, I was invited as a special guest to the Marine Corps Ball by Paul Ramirez's commanding officer, Major Aaron Brooks, back at MATSS-1. The Marine Corps Ball is held in early November every year to celebrate the "birthday" of the Corps on November 10, 1775; it is the biggest annual social event on every Marine's calendar. It was exciting to make one of my first official Marine Corps appearances back in Mississippi, where I was born. It was actually the first ball I had ever gotten to attend, since I was in Cuba for my first Marine Corps birthday and in Afghanistan for my second. It was also one of my first major trips since the injury that had nothing at all to do with medical care. Yes, I was invited to speak—one of the first times I had gotten to do so publicly—and seated at the head table, but I also just got to be Lance Corporal Carpenter, hanging out with other Marines in my dress blues on the dance floor.

The ball was held at a casino, and some of the Marines taught me how to play roulette. The CO explained the rules and offered to do the buy-in for five numbers. "How do you choose?" I asked.

"A lot of people just go for birth dates or other significant dates," he explained.

I couldn't think of a more significant day than when I fell on the grenade, November 21. Then I added my and my parents' birthdays, and the month I woke up. I had my five.

The ball launched and rattled around the wheel until it finally dropped into a slot.

"Twenty-one!" the dealer called.

Major Brooks turned to me with huge eyes: "You won! Twenty-one hit!"

"Aw, man," I cracked. "I'm tired of getting hit on twenty-one!"

And that was the direction life was going for me. I was able to make jokes about what happened—and not just with Stinson about his grenade pepper shaker. Yes, the act that caused such severe injury to Nick and to me was horrible and changed us forever. But with every new experience and every new choice I made, that terrible act lost some of its power.

One of the biggest benefits of the WWR was its connection with people in the "outside world" who could help us find opportunities for professional development and meaningful engagement with our communities. Paul was a huge advocate for his guys, chasing down leads to help us volunteer and meet dynamic people in the fields we were interested in pursuing post-military. When he learned I had been a football player and would love to coach someday, Paul reached out to someone who was buddies with the head coach of Georgetown football and arranged for me to attend practice several times a week as a chance to get out of the hospital, see what coaching was like, and just spend time around other people. I loved getting to experience football from the "other side" instead of as a player, and my respect for coaches and the leadership it takes to manage a team with so many different personalities and styles grew immensely. That arrangement only lasted a few weeks until my next surgery, but it left me feeling excited about possibilities for my future.

Paul was just another example of how one person who is willing to make a connection can completely change someone's outlook, attitude, and sense of hope. He had really listened to my interests and tried to honor my goals. His friend had put me in touch with the coach. And the coach had welcomed a young Marine with zero coaching experience to his practices, and had shared his wisdom and experience with me. Any one of those people could have easily shot down my dream; it seemed improbable that I'd ever be able to work as a coach in the kind of condition I was in. But no one chose to see it that way, and it was yet another lesson to me in the value of living outwardly, agreeing to the unknown, and taking the risk.

Over New Year's, several of us from my regiment flew to Chicago for a weekend away from the hospital to attend a Chicago Bulls game. The trip was short, but it was important symbolically. We were able to do the sorts of things we would have been doing if we hadn't been injured—just being young guys in our twenties, having a good time and celebrating all the promise and potential that the new year holds. We were living out hope, and that was empowering.

I was also thrilled to learn that Nick had returned to Walter Reed for continued care. For a variety of reasons, we weren't able to spend as much time visiting as I would have liked, but it was encouraging to see that he, and so many other guys we didn't even know, were on the same journey: We were reclaiming our lives and learning how to be our fullest selves, not in spite of our injuries but because of them. Our injuries happened. Nothing would ever change that. Our wounds were a part of our bodies, but we were the ones who got to choose what part they played in our stories.

That spring, I was presented the opportunity to participate in the Marine Corps Mud Run. My parents had been adamantly against my skydiving but they just shook their heads and prayed when I went ahead and jumped out of the airplane. But the Mud Run was different. There were countless opportunities for me to fall off the obstacles, which were wet, slippery, and high, which put me in particular danger. My arm had been fractured in thirty places and even though Dr. Newman had defied the odds and been able to salvage it, he had also warned me that if I ever broke it again, it would be nearly impossible to save it a second time.

So Mom and Dad worried that I was risking losing an arm just for the sake of a few hours of fun. They both begged me to reconsider, and I really did try to think about what they said, but in the end, I knew that the potential risk was worth the reward.

"If I let the fear of getting hurt again stop me from doing this," I told them, "what else will I not do in life because of fear or not knowing what could happen?"

As they did when I told them about my intention to join the Marine Corps, Mom and Dad eventually accepted my decision, then quickly became my loudest fans.

The run was disgusting—muddy and grueling and exhausting—and everything I had hoped for. Looking back at how slippery the obstacles were and how weak my grip was, I can admit now that maybe my parents were right that it was too much of a risk. But it was a risk that at the time I felt I had to take. I loved the feeling of pushing my body in ways I hadn't in almost a year and a half. I had to climb walls and crawl through tunnels and do a hundred other things I wouldn't have thought twice about before the grenade, but every obstacle now took on a whole new significance—and every time I conquered one, I took on new significance, too.

I gained significance as someone who fought to live and was succeeding.

I gained significance as a combat survivor who was doing more than just surviving.

I gained significance as someone who attacked physical and occupational therapy with every fiber of my being and was now proving what my restored body could do.

I gained significance as someone who refused to let fear make his choices for him.

I gained significance as someone who reclaimed his life unapologetically.

And even if that significance was only apparent to me, and no one else, it changed who I was in my own eyes and in my own mind. (Oh—and my arm did fine!)

My injuries will not define my life: I will. And the greatest power I have—that any of us has—is the power to make that choice. I have skydived twice since that first day when I went out with Jumping for a Purpose. It still terrifies me, but I do it anyway because when I feel my heart pounding in my chest, it reminds me that I am still alive and that that very heartbeat had stopped before—twice.

Chapter 13
Don't Hide Your Scars

One of the toughest things about recovery is the monotony. As much as you grow to respect and even love your health-care team, it can get tiring to see the same people every day as you go through the same routine. Even when you get new nurses, the schedule doesn't vary much. You get a surgery, you rest. You go to physical therapy, you rest. You go to occupational therapy, you rest. You eat hospital food, you dream of eating . . . well, anything else. By the spring of 2012, I could leave the hospital grounds, which was fantastic, but I was still living at Walter Reed, and that was getting a little old. Which was why, when Carlos Toranzo gave me a call and said that he was at home on leave and wanted to see me if I felt up to it, I couldn't have agreed faster. Not only did I miss him and the rest of the boys, I was excited to catch up. It was also just a welcome break from hospital life. I was eager for anything that was different. I had no idea just how different an experience I was in for.

I had become close with Toranzo in Afghanistan. He came from one of the roughest neighborhoods in the D.C. area, and when I would sit post at night, he would come talk to me and tell me crazy stories from back home, including one in which he had almost been stabbed to death. He still had the scar on his neck. I couldn't imagine what his childhood had been like, and I know he couldn't imagine mine, either: a series of small Southern towns with a stable home and never a brush with the law. Those conversations were eye-opening for me, and made me realize how my seemingly boring, uneventful life was actually pretty extraordinary—for its lack of dysfunction, if nothing else. Toranzo would describe his scrapes with fellow gang members and encounters with the police, how he had joined the Marine Corps in part as an alternative to the gang life, and had had to leave his friends behind in the process. Toranzo enlisted in the Marines, in a way, to avoid ending up dead, but also because he was a U.S. resident at the time and wanted to serve the country that had allowed him and his family a path toward citizenship and a better life. It made me think more about the reasons *I* had enlisted: to be a part of something bigger than myself and to feel I had really lived. I was amazed at the different paths that had brought us to the same place.

I went to meet Toranzo at a local bar called Union Jack's. It was only about a mile away in a neat little center with restaurants and shops in downtown Bethesda, and I usually walked there when I wanted to get out, but that evening I took a cab. I must have had a long day at therapy because I remember feeling a little worn out, and I spent half the ride worried that Toranzo would rag on me about taking a taxi for such a short distance after all the miles we'd hiked together.

When I arrived, I was surprised to see he wasn't alone; he had brought a few of his buddies from his old life with him—buddies who were active gang members. When he introduced them, I learned that these were childhood friends, and among the few guys from his past Toranzo felt he could hang around safely. They were some of the toughest-looking dudes I had ever seen in my life—heavily tattooed, and it looked as if a dozen past fights were mapped out on their bodies in scars. They seemed like the sort to never acknowledge you unless you were in with them or you crossed them. I definitely didn't want to be or do either. I'm not going to lie: I was a little intimidated.

But there I was, sitting in a faux-British pub, chatting with some guys from a completely different world than I had ever known. A world so far removed from my small-town upbringing, I could barely wrap my head around it. I'm not even sure how I introduced myself, because what do you say? "Pleased to meet you, Mr. Gang Member, sir" doesn't exactly cut it. But the awkwardness lasted all of two seconds before one of them started shaking my hand and the other put his arm around me. They told me they had wanted to come and meet me because of what Toranzo had described to them about everything that went down during our deployment, and my injury. "You've been through some shit for your brother, *vato*," one guy said, "so you're our brother forever and we are always here for you."

And just like that, the ice broke and we were just four guys laughing and talking in a bar. They told me they respected everything I did and what I was going through, and that if they were ever in a position to protect someone, they hoped they could do the same thing for their brothers. That evening, I came to understand a little bit more about Toranzo and the influences that had shaped him, and I came to realize why he was such a good Marine: He had grown up surrounded by a code of toughness, loyalty, and community. The street was a little different from the military, but some of the principles were the same. And when those guys, who had been through stuff I could never even imagine, recognized someone else who had lived through hell, they felt a connection. None of our stories was pretty, and we carried the marks from them on our bodies as reminders of what we'd been through. It was all a little crazy; gang members generally don't go around giving hugs to people, but what I came to realize was that my scars somehow seemed to bridge the otherwise large gap between us.

Scars, it turns out, are a universal language. One of the most unexpected parts of the rebuilding process was the connection I forged with people who otherwise might have been invisible to me. I've had homeless people strike up conversations, parolees say hello, and guys who had been raised on the streets talking to me as if I were one of their own. They often can't relate to the stable, middle-class upbringing I've experienced any more than I can relate to the hard life they've had, but we both understand pain and brokenness. We have a bond . . . through our scars.

Not long ago, I was walking in downtown Columbia, South Carolina, when I passed two homeless men talking on the street. I'd just come from a meeting and was dressed up, and one of the men said, kindly, "Looking sharp, brother!" I thanked him as (I admit) I waited for the follow-up question of if I had any money. But as I continued walking nothing else was said. I reached my car but I couldn't shake him from my mind. Half of my brain was telling me to turn around and talk to him, and the other half was telling me just to forget about it and drive away. I stood there with the car door open, wrestling with myself over what I should do. It seemed silly to walk all the way back there, but I couldn't get in my car. I didn't really know what I was doing but I thought to myself, *What if this is the last time you ever see that nice man?*

I closed the door and walked back up the hill. The second man had left but the one who had spoken to me was still there. I apologized to him that I did not have any cash, but I offered to take him to a nearby store for some snacks and supplies. He thanked me and shook my hand. His name was Kenny. His only request was a pack of cigarettes, though he told me he didn't smoke. I had wanted to buy him food, so I asked him what he needed the cigarettes for if he didn't smoke. I am thankful I was wearing glasses because his answer brought tears to my eyes. He explained to me that "down at the mission these things are gold and I can sell a single cigarette for two dollars." After a little grocery shopping, we sat outside the college mart and talked for another half hour. He asked me about my scars, and I told him about Afghanistan. He showed me some of his scars and shared the stories that went with them—childhood accidents, old work injuries from when he was employed, inevitable marks that come from living on the streets.

Kenny told me he enjoyed speaking with me because even though I was someone who had a different life from his, it was clear that I had experienced extraordinary physical and mental pain. I might not have been sleeping under a bridge, but all it took was one look to know that I'd dealt with hardships that most people from my background had been fortunate enough not to have to face. I think (and hope) that made me more relatable to Kenny, and that he felt he could talk with me openly and honestly. My scars were a kind of credential that proved I was someone who had been through the worst and still managed to survive.

Then there is the greeter at my local Walmart, an elderly gentleman who always has a cheerful hello for everyone who comes through the door. One day, as I was walking in, he spotted me, flashed his huge grin, and then did finger pistols at me as he playfully asked, "Motorcycle wreck?"

I did finger pistols right back at him and replied, "Taliban!"

I certainly wasn't planning on a heart-to-heart with the Walmart greeter that day, but that was what happened as we struck up a conversation about my injuries and recovery, and he told me about some of his most difficult times. It was a simple thing, but in a world where we can feel so disconnected from those around us, he and I had a genuine human moment.

After speeches I often have people come up to talk to me and say, "I recognize your tracheotomy scars on your throat. I had a trach, too." I used to be puzzled by this. But now, when I recognize the signs of a skin graft on someone's arm, I can immediately empathize with the pain they experienced, even if our stories are completely different.

Maybe my perspective on things is a little skewed when I tell people not to hide their scars, since I don't really have a choice in the matter; some of my scars are going to show no matter what I wear. Maybe it is easier not to think about your scars if they are on a part of your body that you can easily cover. And maybe there are those who simply choose not to show their scars. I would never encourage anyone to share something they aren't comfortable sharing. But there are some scars that are so obvious, so apparent, that it is impossible to hide or ignore them. Instead of being ashamed of them, I think there is power in embracing these "stories" that leave their marks on our bodies and souls.

I could choose to hide some of my scars—I can wear long sleeves over the injuries on my arms or long pants to cover my legs—but there is no way to hide the marks on my face. Actually, that's not entirely true. My doctors call them my "gunpowder tattoos." They were caused by the hot pieces of shrapnel laced with explosive powder that seared into my face as they passed through my skin when the grenade detonated, and the way the pigment stained my skin is pretty much the same as with regular tattoos (except for the mode of delivery, of course). As a result, laser tattoo-removal surgery was an option for me, and it actually worked fairly well in a couple of places where I tried it. But the pain was unbelievable: Imagine a rubber band snapping against your skin, nonstop, for an hour or more at a time . . . then multiply that pain by ten. In a healthy patient, lidocaine or a similar numbing agent can be injected into the major nerve centers in the face, and the medicine will then spread to the other nerves until the entire face is numb. The shots are painful, but thankfully, only one or two are necessary for most people. In my case, however, I had to get many more because the nerve connections had all been severed in my face, which meant that the medicine couldn't spread effectively or evenly.

After the second laser treatment, I looked at myself in the mirror through swollen eyelids and couldn't believe what I saw. My face looked like I had been beaten with a Louisville Slugger in a street fight, or like I had stuck it in a beehive. My head felt twice its normal size, and I knew it would take at least a week before the swelling finally went down. It just didn't seem worth it. I told the doctors that I appreciated their work, but it felt like we were trying to buffer out a dent when the car was totaled.

In fact, I passed on all the scar-revision procedures offered to me, aside from those two laser treatments on my face. I could have undergone a scar-revision surgery every week for the next five years, and it would still be immediately obvious to anyone looking at me that my body had been through something awful. I mean, my entire right arm had a skin graft from the shoulder to the hand. No amount of surgery is ever going to conceal that. Besides, erasing the scars felt like erasing what I had been through. I had already come to appreciate the tremendous power that scars have for creating bonds, and that was more important to me than a clear face.

Not to mention that some of the scars are pretty badass. When I launched my Twitter account later in 2012, I chose the handle @chiksdigscars. Because I was hoping they would.

My philosophy on scars took an unexpected turn as I began to make more public appearances, and I soon learned that it wasn't always my physical scars that created intense and sometimes surprising bonds. After attending the Commandant's Marine Corps Birthday Ball with a crowd of several thousand people, I was in the middle of a meet and greet when one Marine whose uniform showed he was a much higher rank than me approached me and started to get choked up. I could tell there was something he wanted to say, so I turned with him so that our backs were to the receiving line and the cameras and we could speak a little more privately. He thanked me for sharing my story and then confessed I was the reason he had not killed himself. If I had survived and fought through all I had endured, he knew he could keep fighting his emotional scars, too.

I hardly knew what to say to that, standing there in the middle of a huge crowd with a few hundred more hands to shake. Finally, I just looked him in the eye and said, "Promise me I'll see you next year."

He smiled a little and said, "Yes. I will see you next year." I gave him a hug and then he was gone, back into the crowd.

The thing about scars is that they bear witness to something in our past. They are a reminder of an incident, an injury, an accident, or a mishap—something that went wrong. But they are also a reminder of something that went right: The body healed itself. It created new tissue around the injury in order to protect it and close it. That can only happen if you are alive; scars mark you as a survivor. And, given enough time, most scars start to fade. Your body has the ability to preserve, protect, and persist.

There is a difference between a wound and a scar. A wound is still fresh; it runs the risk of infection if it's not tended to properly. It can still cause pain. It may need to remain covered until it has healed sufficiently to be exposed. But the time will come to remove the bandage and let sunlight and air do their healing work, too. Only you will know when that time is, but when it comes, I hope you are not afraid or ashamed or embarrassed. Your scars may not be pleasant to look at, but what they represent is a beautiful resilience and a toughness that no one can ever question or take from you.

Wear your scars proudly. Wear them for yourself, to honor what you've been through. And wear them for others, to connect with them and inspire them to keep on fighting. Scars are evidence that injuries can heal and pain can fade. Your scars can give someone the reassurance that they are not alone, and give others the hope that someday, their wounds will become nothing but scars, too.

Chapter 14
"Stay Motivated"

"Stay motivated."

Any Marine reading this is rolling their eyes right now. Those two words, "stay motivated," are pretty well-worn within the Corps. Leadership loves to say them when you're in formation or on a grueling run or anytime there is a lag in the conversation. In fact, it seems like when you are cold and wet and hungry and dirty and missing home, that's when they say it the most: "Stay motivated."

That line has become a bit of a joke that Marines will toss around sarcastically in really miserable situations when it seems everyone hates their life. But still, there is wisdom in the phrase. There are going to be times when you want nothing more in the world than to give up and throw in the towel. But you know that, somehow, you've got to keep pushing forward—even if it's just to take care of the Marines to the right and left of you. That's when the idea of staying motivated really resonates.

It would be easy to look at my story so far and think that I am some kind of unsinkable, eternal optimist who woke up smiling every day in the hospital, jumping out of bed to get to rehab, and never staying down too long when things got tough. I can promise you that was not the case. True, I've always been a naturally positive person, but positivity isn't enough to get you from hour to hour when your entire world has been rocked and you don't know if you'll ever have a pain-free moment again in your life. That's when you need motivation. Positivity is feeling good about the way things will work out in the future; motivation is the drive to *make* things work out.

One of the earliest clear memories I have from when I woke up in the hospital is of a doctor—I don't remember his name or rank or anything about him except that he might have been a resident, since he seemed very young—checking on me once in the middle of the night. I was terribly cold and I could barely let him know, but somehow I managed to communicate that I couldn't get warm. He disappeared and came back about ten minutes later with an armful of blankets and towels, straight out of the dryer. As he tucked them in around me, I felt my body start to calm down from the shivering, and then I fell back asleep.

That's it—a short scene, but it's one of the first things I can recall with any real clarity. I found out later that the hospital laundry wasn't anywhere near my room, but this young doctor went on a personal mission to find something warm to make me more comfortable. He didn't have a nurse do it. He didn't submit a request somewhere and wait. He didn't say, "This guy just got blown up and he's complaining about being cold? Whatever." Or "He'll pass back out again in a few minutes." He saw a need and he set out to meet it. And even in my disoriented state, I understood that there was something wonderful about a person who takes their job so personally that they do whatever is necessary in the moment without passing the buck. That is someone who grasps the fundamental importance of those two seemingly simple words: Stay motivated.

The truth is, motivation is hard. It's hard to get motivated and it's even harder to stay motivated— especially when you have been knocked down lower than you ever imagined possible. During those first months back from Afghanistan, my hospital room was a testament to my *not* being okay: I was on a breathing machine, I was on a feeding tube, I needed at least one (but sometimes two) corpsmen sitting with me every minute of the day to monitor my vitals, known as a "one-to-one." As grateful as I was for these things, there is nothing about a setup like that that projects a message of confidence. In no way does that convey a sense of "You're going to be just fine." Everything communicates, "This guy is barely hanging on." It's so hard to keep your mind fixed on better days ahead when you're still relying on a machine to put oxygen in your body to get you through the night. Then you subconsciously hear the words:

Stay motivated.

Those days were especially hard because well-meaning people want to encourage you. They want to show their support and let you know how much you are appreciated. They want to pray for you and with you. They want you to feel loved. They don't want you to be lonely. And they want to see for themselves that you are going to be okay. And you appreciate that— you truly do. But maybe you're not feeling it that day or that hour or that minute, and you don't want to be rude to the well-wishers but you can't handle one more person seeing you at your worst.

My parents ended up policing my door to the point that my dad said he felt like a bouncer. There were so many people who were there to lift the spirits of injured and ill service members, especially around the holidays, and I know their time and efforts meant a great deal to a lot of people. But I wasn't at a point then where I could receive visitors or make small talk or smile and show appreciation. I was still trying to get a grasp on my own reality; I wasn't ready to welcome other people into my new orbit.

In the end, my parents put up a sign on my door to gently but firmly let people know that I did not want visitors. I had a constant stream of doctors and nurses coming in and out, running tests or checking on something. It's wonderful that political figures and celebrities visit troops, but I didn't need more of a parade of faces and questions than I was already getting. I was still confused, and confusion breeds fear, and fear can breed despair. And even though I was determined not to let on to my family how overwhelming it all was, I'm sure they had to know that I was fighting every day to hang on to the good moments.

When you've been brought that low, you are seeing the world from a whole new perspective—and the bigness of it all can overpower you. And somewhere in your broken, scrambled, mixed-up version of whoever you are right now as you try to rebuild your sense of self, there might be a piece of you who trusts that there is life on the other side of this storm . . . but right now the waves are so tall that you can't see over them.

Stay motivated.

Then, one day, you are feeling good. Something happens that makes you feel like yourself again, and suddenly you start to remember who you are. For me, that was the day I managed to get my body clean. It was my first real shower in six months—since before I deployed. But that day, I finally managed an honest-to-goodness shower with real water pressure. Every bit of Afghan dust and deployment sweat was washed away; all of the hospital residue, whatever that is—some kind of mix of adhesive from bandages and iodine, maybe, and whatever else my skin had accumulated over the past few weeks—everything was scrubbed clean away. It took hours to do it carefully, without dislodging any tubes or getting anything wet that needed to stay dry, but all the effort finally paid off: I was clean. I was sitting in the recliner in my room—sitting upright, which was a major deal by itself. I was happy and warm and clean and the pain wasn't the first thing on my mind. My arms were comfortable. We had arranged my blankets exactly right so that everything was as perfect as I could ever dare hope. I felt like a champion. Like a king.

A new nurse came in—a rookie, fresh out of naval officer school, and eager to do a really great job. She was assigned to feeding me, which involved injecting my "food" with a huge plastic syringe into the feeding tube that went straight into my stomach. As she did so, she realized she hadn't clamped off the tube properly and the contents started spraying all over me—just disgusting muck literally everywhere. I tried to control my emotions to avoid a freak-out—not an angry rage, but a sobbing meltdown like a little kid who has emotionally maxed out. Something in me snapped. "Can you please just leave?" I asked. She kept trying to help clean me up but it was all too much. "Just get out." That was the only time I was ever rude or visibly frustrated with any member of the staff during any of my hospital stays, and I felt horrible about it the moment she left, but I couldn't deal with that disappointment after the temporary high I'd been enjoying.

Fortunately, about five years later, I ran into that same nurse at the Subway in the Walter Reed cafeteria. I recognized her right away and ran up to introduce myself so I could apologize profusely for the way I'd handled the situation. She was gracious and said it was all her fault, and we had a nice conversation in which we both unloaded the guilt we'd been carrying around for years. Most of the time, we don't get those opportunities to make something right after the fact and we have to push ahead, feeling badly.

Life is like that. You manage to pull yourself up from whatever your rock bottom is, and you feel good for a minute before you get knocked right back on your butt again. It could be something that doesn't seem like a big deal to anyone else, but it is devastating for you because of where you've been and how far away you still are from where you want to be. You are frustrated by circumstances and maybe even with yourself for how you reacted. You might be angry, tired, broken, hurt, confused. What can you possibly do in a situation like that?

Stay motivated.

Crisis mode can last a few hours, or a few months. And the longer you are in that mode, the more exhausting it is. No matter what promises you hear that things are going to get better, they are still just promises. What is real is what is happening right now, and right now you are suffering like you've never experienced suffering before.

I remember how painful every little movement was for a very long time—even while I was sleeping. Sometimes during the day I would drift off due to the pain meds, but when it came time to actually sleep at night, the pain was inescapable. My lymph nodes were so swollen that it ached to lift my arms even the slightest bit, and I had to undergo a fasciotomy, where the limb has to be sliced open to relieve pressure, due to the fact that my right arm was so swollen that it was starting to cut off the circulation to the good tissue that remained.

At Bethesda, I was on pain medicine the whole time. Once, a few days after a thirteen-hour surgery to try to repair my arm, there was about a thirty-minute delay in refreshing my pain meds. That was when the hospital was at its most overcrowded, and no one was able to get in to start the next dose before the level of pain blockers in my system started to drop. To fix the thirty fractures in my arm, they had inserted a metal rod through each of the main three bones in it. The pain radiated from deep in the core of my bones. It was one of the most excruciating experiences of my life, and I honestly thought I was going to pass out. But that was the only time I was fully aware of the level of pain my body was actually going through. The rest of the time, medicine dulled it.

The very worst feeling, however, was breathing. They had inserted a trach and with that, you feel like you are getting only about 70 percent of the air you want because you aren't used to getting oxygen through a tube in your throat. I vividly remember trying to take slow, deep breaths so I could fill my lungs completely . . . but even that was mentally treacherous because with a trach, you encounter the same amount of resistance breathing in as you do forcing air out. By the time I could release the full breaths I had taken, I was already starting to panic about being able to suck air back in. Who knew breathing could be so stressful? I wasn't as sedated anymore and there were times when I would start to panic, thinking I was running out of air, and would blow the cap off the hole in my neck. Then I would really start to panic but I couldn't move because I was surrounded by so many machines and feeling claustrophobic, even though I was in a huge room. I was in severe pain, breathing through a straw, and it felt like the walls were closing in.

Once I got to Richmond, there were new discomforts. They were tapering my pain medication, plus I had other complications, like bedsores. No matter how diligent the care team was in trying to prevent them, bedsores were pretty much guaranteed, since in my condition I couldn't shift position.

Thankfully, I had an amazing therapist who was kind and dedicated. One of his most valuable skills was calming me down when I started panicking about the trach. He would try to keep me distracted so that I couldn't fixate on the things that were freaking me out. He never let me stay in my panic; he worked tirelessly to make sure I was taking baby steps forward even through the worst pain I could imagine. He understood the value in trying to push beyond my immediate fears to get to something better. After all, what else could I do?

Stay motivated.

Every now and then, in the midst of those dark valleys in life, you get a wonderful moment that reminds you of everything good in the world. And you can live off those moments for weeks.

Just a few days before I was discharged from the VA hospital, 2/9 got back from deployment. Before going home, my buddies loaded up in the car and drove five hours to Richmond to visit me for a couple of days. They brought with them my Combat Action Ribbon to put on my uniform. "You earned this," Griffin Welch said, "so we wanted to give it to you in person."

That visit was one of the best moments since I had awakened in Bethesda, and it did more to lift my spirits and give me the power to keep going than just about anything else. I knew I wasn't forgotten. I knew those hallucinations of my friends turning their backs on me weren't real. I knew I still mattered to them. I knew my life had impacted other people.

Sometimes, even the simplest act, like jumping in a car, delivering something by hand, looking a person in the eye, and simply being there can be every bit as healing as whatever the doctors are doing. It helps you stay connected to life outside your own immediate world. It helps to keep you looking ahead.

Stay motivated.

The last thing I had to do before being discharged from the VA hospital in Richmond was a series of blood draws. The problem was that after three straight months of surgery every other day, I did not have one good vein left from my head to my toes. The phlebotomists started with my arm, poking and repoking, trying to get a decent vein for the draw, but they didn't have any luck; the two of them took turns brainstorming and resticking me in different places. For nearly three hours, they worked their way around my body, even down to the tops of my feet and insides of my ankles. They felt almost as badly about it as I did, and they kept apologizing for how much it hurt.

I will never know how I managed to sit still through it all, but I just kept reminding myself that this was my way out of Richmond, and once I got out of Richmond, my inpatient days were over for a long time.

I might be on the couch all day, every day, at home but I'm going to be living good, I reminded myself. *I'm gonna be with the dog, I'm gonna be watching TV. If I want to watch movies and be lazy, I can do that.*

And I'll be eating Mom's cooking. And I'll be with my family all the time. Grin and bear it. Just get through the next stick. This next one has got to be it. This next one is your ticket out of here. You don't have to spend one more night in this hospital . . .

It was awful, and it seemed like it would never end. As badly as I wanted to give up and tell them to wait until my veins had healed enough to get a decent stick, I forced myself to focus on the end goal, which was going home. Because sometimes, that's all you can do. No matter who you are or where you are in life, there are simply things that are going to be terrible—but you just have to lower your head, put one foot in front of the other, and walk straight into that storm.

Stay motivated.

When so much of what you knew about yourself has been torn away, you look for anything to reassert control over your identity, and you sometimes have to take the long view even when an easier option is available to you.

In my case, the long view involved getting off the pain meds as quickly as possible—and probably sooner and faster than was medically advisable. One of the primary medications I was on, aside from fentanyl patches, gabapentin, and Dilaudid, was methadone, which is what they give to people coming off heroin. It's essentially pharmaceutical heroin. My meds were always prescribed in safe doses and I was never slamming massive amounts of them, but I also recognized that they were very strong drugs and that when I was at home during recovery, it would be easy to turn to them if I needed relief or rest—and I never wanted that to become a temptation.

Plus, I know those drugs aren't easy on your liver and I figured my system had been through enough as it was; I probably shouldn't make my internal organs work any harder than they needed to. I also wanted to be able to better gauge how hard I was pushing myself—could I work harder? Was I working too hard? If I could establish a baseline of pain, I could listen to my own body better in order to match my physical rehab to where my body actually was. So I decided to wean myself off my pain medications. *All* my pain medications.

Some were easy, like gabapentin; it had never done much for me anyway, and when I quit it I didn't have any withdrawal symptoms. But other drugs were much tougher. About two months after I got back to South Carolina, I brought myself off methadone over the course of a week and a half, taking smaller and smaller doses each day while it worked its way slowly and miserably out of my system. It was a week of pure misery. I would lie on the couch and even cry at times. It wasn't just that the pain was increasing every day as my brain became more and more cognizant of all the trauma in my body, but I also had detox tremors—the sweats and the shakes. As the effects of the methadone waned, my body ached to the core of my fractured bones, and as badly as I wanted to change positions to get more comfortable, I couldn't because my arms had to be kept propped up in exactly the right way. I was stuck as my body rebelled against everything it was going through. But in the end, I won that struggle.

By the time I moved back up to Walter Reed in September, I was off everything except the Dilaudid that I needed after surgery. I was incredibly proud of that accomplishment, but as time went on, something started to gnaw at me. There were periods between surgeries when the pain dimmed enough that I could probably have just taken an over-the-counter medication to make it manageable . . . but I found myself reaching for Dilaudid instead because it didn't just take the pain away, it actually made me feel good. The moment I realized that I was starting to enjoy it, I picked up the bottle holding the last of my Dilaudid prescription—probably twelve or fifteen pills left in the bottle—and I threw it away. I did not request a refill. That was early 2012, when I knew I was getting toward the end of my regular surgeries. I didn't want that little stash to be a temptation so I tossed it and never looked back.

Sometimes you make decisions on behalf of Future You. You know that Present You is probably going to have to deal with a little more discomfort or inconvenience right now, but long-term, you will be grateful for the choices you made today. You don't want merely to hope for better days ahead, you want to take the steps necessary to ensure them.

Stay motivated.

You start to emerge from a dark place and you begin to feel your fight coming back to you. But you still have a long ways to go to get back to that good place. Part of the fight is learning to assert yourself again—knowing when to accept graciously what is offered and knowing when to dig in your heels.

The bulk of my time at Walter Reed was focused on facial and oral reconstructive surgery. Most people think you get injured, the surgeons open you up, put you back together, and that is that. In some cases, this is true. But in more complex cases, the time line is longer. You have to make sure the bones are healing the right way; you have to make sure there is good blood flow and that vessels are repairing; you have to make sure that the muscles and tendons and other soft tissue are all connected in a manner that makes the body part at least somewhat usable; you have to make sure that the nerve endings are firing like they are supposed to—and each of those stages takes time.

My facial reconstruction really began in Afghanistan, when they tried to salvage what they could of my jaw. After that, the surgeries became more intense and more specific. The surgeons needed to operate on all of the tissues surrounding my bottom lip to rearrange them, because when the first trauma team had sewn the injury closed in order to preserve what was left of my jaw area, my bottom lip had fused to where my teeth had been because there was nothing to prop it up. I had to go through gum and tissue surgery to remove my bottom lip from the lower bridge of my mouth, and it was one of the most painful surgeries of all. A hard plastic mouthpiece had to be screwed in place for two weeks to help my bottom lip and soft tissue re-form. Every time I tried to move my tongue, the piece sliced my mouth. I hated that thing, but I understood we had to go through each step of the process before we could begin the next one. And the oral-maxillofacial surgeons were honest with me that, even after all that pain and reconstructive work, I still might never have normal teeth again because I had lost so much bone that they weren't even sure what they could secure them to.

Most of my face, from my eye sockets down, is titanium now. An X-ray from early on looks almost like someone shot a glitter gun at my face, because all you can see on the lower half of it are thousands of tiny pieces of bone scattered everywhere. Six months after the injury, my doctors were shocked and thrilled to find that so much bone had grown back—more than they anticipated—but they were concerned about causing further damage to what little soft tissue I had remaining by drilling into that new bone to try to set dental implants in place.

It was depressing news, to say the least.

But right at the time that I was finally eligible to get the first implants inserted to see if they would hold, some new technology emerged that looked like it could greatly increase the odds of a successful dental reconstruction. Unfortunately, it was still experimental, which meant lots of red tape, and the procedure kept getting delayed. Everyone was frustrated. Finally, I sat down with an Army colonel who was head of the dental clinic at Walter Reed and explained that I wasn't going to wait much longer. Either they purchased and acquired the technology needed to perform my surgery, or I was going to get the procedure done elsewhere, outside the military system. He went to bat for me, and one month later, I was finally wheeled into surgery.

I now have a functioning jaw and full set of teeth. And that experimental machine has become a permanent reconstructive tool at Walter Reed. I can carry with me the knowledge that part of the good that came out of my experience is that I could help further the treatments available to other injured service members who would come after me.

Stay motivated.

You keep nudging, creeping, and stumbling forward because that's the only option you have: forward or backward.

One surgery rerouted a tendon from my arm up around my wrist so that I could finally bend my wrist upward. It had been such a major victory just to get to neutral; now I was actually lifting my hand up from my arm! It may not sound like much, but I knew everything it had taken to get to that point, and those seemingly small victories were anything but insignificant.

I had my official rehab, and what I called my unofficial rehab. I would work with my incredible therapists, and then I would take what we did together and I would push myself further in between sessions. Even as I was working on recapturing the ability to perform fine motor skills with my hands, I was also looking for ways to push myself physically to regain my overall strength and fitness, too.

I hate running. But every two weeks or so, when I was at Walter Reed, I would dare myself to do something big, and I'd go on a run to the Capitol and back—five miles round-trip. I couldn't risk nerve damage to my arms from weight-lifting and I wanted to get myself back into fighting shape, so I had to take the route available to me. My legs didn't sustain any serious tissue or nerve damage, so there was my solution.

People were concerned, obviously, when I would be outside in ninety-degree heat and humidity for a jog I could have easily done on a treadmill, but that was part of the deal I had with myself not to quit. I could have stopped at any time on a treadmill if it got uncomfortable, but if I was out, I had to get myself back to the hospital, one way or another. I took away my excuse for quitting, and I found my own incentive.

Stay motivated.

People start to question if your sacrifice was really worth it, and you have to remind yourself of the stories that no one else saw.

There was a local Afghan boy, about twelve, who loved the Marines and would always salute us when we would walk out of our patrol base on foot. He and his eight-year-old brother even made a game of trying to snatch water bottles and goodies from the "dump pouches" on the back of our SAPI (small arms protective insert) plates, which were designed to carry empty magazines from firefights but doubled as snack, candy, and water bottle carriers. The two boys got to be friends with us, and through the months of talking and playing with us would sometimes tell us where well-hidden IEDs were buried. Our EOD (explosive ordnance disposal) guys made a good show of trying to make it appear that their discoveries were accidental before the explosives were defused, but in Taliban strongholds, eyes are always watching.

One night, about two weeks after I was evacuated, a grenade was thrown over the wall of our compound and detonated at exactly the spot where my now-empty bunk sat. No one was injured, but it obviously shook everyone up a bit. A few nights later, that same boy who used to salute us showed up at our patrol base in the middle of the night to tell us he threw that grenade. He was sobbing and begging the Marines to forgive him and not to kill him. The Taliban had caught on that he was friendly with us and that fewer IEDs were being detonated. They suspected he was the cause, so they beat him senseless—but they didn't kill him. Instead, for his final punishment, they dragged him to the wall of our compound, placed a grenade in his hand, and pulled the pin. A twelve-year-old child was forced to kill or be killed.

That was just one story of countless others we heard—stories of violence, ritual stoning of women, pushing people off buildings for being gay. And children forced to become weapons of war.

How is one not affected witnessing that degree of evil? You remind yourself why you were over there in the first place—to put a stop to the Taliban and their torture and oppression of their own people. You remind yourself that, if you were able to weaken their stronghold or just give hope to those innocent people, even in the smallest of ways, so that one day they might taste the freedom of safety, then you made a difference.

That helps you stay focused.

That helps you *stay motivated.*

Life looks different on the other side of a tragedy. The things you once valued have changed. The things you once believed in are scrambled. The things you focused on from day to day are different now. Not everyone understands this. You are still you, but you aren't exactly the same and you never will be again.

There are still times when I wake up with the terrifying realization that I could have taken my last breath at twenty-one years old. I would not have experienced jumping off a ninety-foot cliff, going skydiving, riding in a hot air balloon. I would have never seen my family again, or earned my place in the world, or been able to just sit around and watch college football with my brothers.

The official report showed that the grenade impacted me on the upper right quadrant of my abdomen, just below my heart and right over my lungs, which explains why my right lung was fully collapsed. It seems to have caught the corner of my SAPI plate, which is bulletproof armor designed to withstand seven rounds of a 7.62-millimeter caliber, which is akin to a round fired from an AK-47—in other words, a pretty decent-size round. That is an *incredible* amount of impact through which the plate can maintain its structural integrity, but when one of my friends from 2/9 picked up my SAPI plate after the explosion, he said it was like a bag full of shattered glass; its armor pieces just fell to the bottom of the plate carrier. The armor had done its job, splintering inside the casing, and that was what prevented me from being blown literally in half. The nylon tourniquet I had been carrying—we all had them in case of emergencies—had melted onto the SAPI plate carrier, and the carrier, along with my body, was smoking. There was almost nothing left of my weapon at all. To be honest, there wasn't much left of me, either. But I'm still here.

It can be easy to marvel at the big things but get discouraged by the little things. Just because I am a positive person and optimistic about my future doesn't mean that I don't have worries, too. My ears still ring so loudly that it's often difficult to concentrate; it's hard sometimes not to feel overwhelmed that my ears are almost certainly going to ring like that forever. I don't have two eyes or 20/20 vision anymore; the world will literally never look the same. I'm never going to be able to do some basic tasks, like put on a suit, without a little help.

I try to focus on the fact that new technologies are coming out every year that can make a difference for people like me. I hold tight to the hope that these medical breakthroughs will be able to help me out as I age. I try to keep the faith that these things that seem like permanent challenges for me now might not be down the road. Yes, I try to be positive, but it's not all thumbs-up, big-smile-all-the-time. It's tough living with the consequences of what happened . . . but at the same time, there is no question that the positives outweigh the negatives. I've done more with my life now, a hundred times more, than I ever did before I was injured.

You change. The people around you change. Relationships change. Even your understanding of God changes. Everything changes. But you are supposed to stay motivated . . . for what? For a future that is still totally unclear? For a life that some people have decided is too much for them to handle? For all the people who didn't get this second chance? Maybe.

Stay motivated.

Wisdom comes with time, and perspective comes with distance. Sometimes you feel overwhelmed by the extraordinary turn your life has taken, and sometimes you are caught completely off guard by a phone call on a seemingly normal night.

One evening in early spring 2012, I was enjoying dinner at a Mexican restaurant in Bethesda called Guapo's when my phone rang. I was at a booth in the back with a couple of buddies, and I had trouble hearing the person on the other end because of the noise in the restaurant and the mariachi music blaring over the speakers. Eventually, I was able to make out that the caller said his name was Chief Warrant Officer Reeves.

"Do you have a minute to talk?" he asked. "I just want to ask you a couple questions about the day you were injured."

"Okay," I replied. "Can you please hold just one minute, sir?"

I signaled to my friends that I needed to take this call, and went outside.

CWO-5 Reeves proceeded to tell me that he had been assigned to 2/9 to lead the investigation into the circumstances surrounding my injury to determine whether a Medal of Honor might be considered for my actions on the roof.

The first thing he wanted to know was what I remembered about the events leading up to the grenade. Since my memory of the day ended with Nick and me discussing how quickly we'd get *off* the roof if a grenade landed up there, I had to be honest with him.

"Unfortunately, I'm sorry, sir, but I do not remember any of the events leading up to it," I said.

I explained how the only thing I could recall was that I felt myself on my knees, falling forward, a few inches from the ground. Then it seemed like I was hit really hard in the face. I didn't hear, see, or have any cognizant thoughts about a grenade before the explosion. I didn't understand at the time why I was falling forward and it didn't register in my conscious brain that there had been a grenade. But that wasn't anything that could help him out. "I'm sorry," I repeated. "I just don't remember anything."

He thanked me for my honesty and added, "Two-nine is proud of you no matter the outcome of this investigation. I appreciate you talking with me." And then the call ended.

When I went back into the restaurant, my friends wanted to know what the call was about. They started freaking out as I recounted it. "Dude, are you serious?!?" Paul Ramirez demanded. "They must really be taking this seriously to be starting an investigation!"

I just shrugged. I couldn't imagine it would go anywhere, since I didn't remember anything and couldn't supply any helpful details. I had no idea that every other guy I had been with at PB Dakota was about to be interviewed and interrogated for witness statements, and that the scene would be pored over by every explosive expert and medical professional the military could throw at it. All I knew was that, right now, my dinner was getting cold, so I'd better focus on eating.

It's funny how life-changing conversations can happen in the most ordinary places, like on the sidewalk in front of a Mexican restaurant as you stare across the road at a strip mall. And even though you don't believe the big idea or grand gesture will go anywhere, you're still honored that someone is looking into it, and maybe that feeling sustains you through an especially tough physical therapy session the next day.

Stay motivated.

Stay motivated. It gets old. It gets predictable. It becomes cliché. But in the end, it's good advice. And sometimes, you don't need platitudes or well-wishes or rousing speeches or photo ops, you just need to remember to take the step right in front of you and keep pushing forward, come what may. Honors and awards are great, but they don't always happen—you have to keep moving forward anyway. Recognition is nice, but it can't sustain you—you have to keep plugging away on the awful days as well as the great ones. You have to keep trying. You have to keep hanging on, even when there doesn't seem to be any reason to stick to it. You have to find that reason within yourself.

You have to stay motivated.

Chapter 15
Know Your Worth

Three years after stuffing what I needed into a backpack and shipping out to Afghanistan, life came full circle. I heaved a different pack onto my back, and started out on my next four-year commitment—one very different from the Marine Corps. I enrolled at the University of South Carolina.

As my surgeries became less frequent and I progressed through the levels of my physical therapy, my time at Walter Reed came to a close. The last few months, I was even able to move out of the barracks and into a nearby apartment to practice living on my own. I applied for a top-secret clearance and was granted an internship at the National Counterterrorism Center, which was a phenomenal experience. Through that job, I developed a deep appreciation for foreign policy, diplomacy, and counterterrorism work. This, I knew, was what I wanted to do with my life—which meant I had to lay the necessary groundwork for my new future.

When the question of medical retirement from the Marine Corps was raised, I thought long and hard about it before I decided to go that route. I joined the Marine Corps to contribute to something greater than myself, but I only served on active duty for a year and a half. There was a part of me that loved the idea of a twenty-year career, and I had even started looking to see if there was any possibility that I could become a drill instructor. In some ways, I felt as if I hadn't made any mark at all in such a short time. But on the other hand, I had accomplished what I set out to do. I would always be a Marine, even when I hung up the uniform. I would always be connected to the Marines with whom I served, with whom I was injured, and with whom I recovered. And in the course of all of that, I had discovered my professional calling in counterterrorism work. In the end, I felt like there was life waiting for me outside of the Marine Corps, so I decided to accept the medical retirement option in July 2013.

The ceremony took place in the lobby of Building 62 on the Walter Reed campus. All of the tables were moved out and the American and Marine Corps flags set up along the windows. It wasn't anything dramatic; we had a small reception right there with my family, a couple of buddies, and my Marine Corps leadership from Wounded Warrior Battalion. I didn't want anything big; I wanted to pay honor to that chapter in my life and move on to the next.

Two weeks later, I was walking to class to begin my career as a college student.

My parents had so wanted me to go to college straight out of high school and I had been dead set against it—and yet, as I looked ahead to my life post–Marine Corps, I realized that college was exactly where I wanted to be. I'm not going to lie: There was some culture shock. I didn't understand how some of my classmates could have the seemingly superficial priorities they had, or how they could hold such staunch views and limited perspectives on areas where they had no experience. I couldn't wrap my mind around the fact that some were so mature and others seemed to live in worlds defined by such shallow criteria. But what I quickly came to realize was that I needed to cut them some slack for not having had the same experiences I did, just as much as they probably had to accommodate my transition back into the world of class schedules and homework.

The next seven semesters would teach me to recognize my worth, the worthiness of my experiences, and the worthiness of the unique experiences of the people around me. I think a lot of people—especially nontraditional students who don't start college immediately following high school—struggle with feeling out of place. It can be really difficult to transition from carrying a rifle through the canals and farmlands of southern Afghanistan to carrying books between classes, or to go from having a full-time career to sitting at a desk taking notes. It can be easy to dismiss your classmates as "kids" who live in a bubble and have no idea what the real world is like. But what I found was that we all bring something to the table and learn from one another. That probably sounds a little simplistic and idealistic, but it's important. It's easy to slip into thinking that your perspective is the only one worth anything.

One of my first and most influential classes was History 468, a military history survey course with Dr. Dik Daso. I was excited to take the class because I love history and Dr. Daso had a fascinating background; he was retired from the Air Force and had worked as the curator of modern military aircraft at the National Air and Space Museum in Washington, D.C., before moving to South Carolina. I figured he would have an interesting angle on military history and that I would have a different appreciation for it.

What I didn't realize was that Dr. Daso had worked for two years as one of the curators for an exhibit called "The Price of Freedom" at the Smithsonian National Museum of American History, and one of his tasks was to interact with the Medal of Honor Society to help create the content for an interactive kiosk that told the stories of Medal of Honor recipients. As a result of working on that project, he became aware of a number of service members or veterans who were under consideration for the Medal of Honor, one of whom was me. When he saw my name on his class roster, he was curious as to whether I was the same William Kyle Carpenter from South Carolina he had heard about; either way, he was certain there was a story behind my scars, so he did some research. Finally, about five class sessions into the semester, he asked me to stay after class.

"Kyle," he said, "you're a nominee for the Medal of Honor?"

I wasn't quite sure what he was getting at, so I decided just to answer honestly: "Yes, sir. I know."

He paused a second, then asked, "You know you're going to get that medal, don't you?"

I didn't understand where his confidence came from, so I just shrugged and smiled, saying, "Ah, well, I don't know. The investigation is still under way."

"Trust me, I used to work at the Pentagon, and investigations don't get as far down the road as yours is without there being something to it," he assured me. "It's pretty clear to me it's just a matter of time."

I appreciated his confidence, but I didn't hold the same belief that it was almost a sure thing. But after that meeting, we shared a kind of bond. He knew I didn't want to make a big deal out of my service record, but he also understood that I was coming at the classroom experience from a different place than most of my peers. Finally, toward the end of the semester, on Veterans Day, he read a one-page summary of the grenade attack but without naming me. The other students listened attentively as he described what happened, but then, at the very end, Dr. Daso said, "And, by the way, this is about Kyle Carpenter. He's one of your schoolmates." And he nodded to where I was sitting. It was a little overwhelming to have a lecture hall full of students suddenly congratulating me and saying thank you, but it was also reassuring to feel so welcomed and celebrated by my peers. It made me realize that maybe I wasn't so out of place after all.

I started to find my way, feeling less isolated and more a part of campus life. I enjoyed my classes and the community of students; I decided to join a fraternity and pledged Kappa Sigma. The college experience my parents had envisioned for me after high school was finally happening.

Still, old habits are hard to break, and "Corporal Carpenter" remained a very real part of "college student Kyle's" life. My roommate, a friend from back home named Preston Doyle, always laughed at my compulsive ironing, a holdover from the military. Any time I was laying out my clothes or getting dressed, I would pull out an ironing board and make sure everything was neatly pressed—even T-shirts and shorts. Eventually I just left it out because I got tired of setting it up every day. I'll admit that may have been a little excessive, but it was the Marine mentality that really helped me juggle all my competing responsibilities and obligations.

As requests for speeches for far-flung corporations and organizations started coming in, I had to figure out how to also keep up with my schoolwork. I woke up early almost every morning to cram as much studying in as I could before my classes started and ahead of the weekend. Sleep deprivation aside, it was kind of nice having the library to myself the first few hours every morning, before the sun and students started to pour in. Many Friday afternoons saw me flying across the country to one speech or another, before I returned home on Sunday and headed straight to the library.

There were a few times when I had to be gone for a week to travel to an American embassy in Europe or the Middle East to talk with the employees and Marine security guards there, but all of my professors were willing to work with me and allow me to make up tests or quizzes or hand in papers early. As long as I was willing to put in the work, they were willing to accommodate my schedule's unusual demands.

There was another side to my growing notoriety, though, which was that I lost a lot of privacy. As my story began to get more press coverage, especially locally, people started to recognize me. Even if people didn't recognize my face, I think my visible injuries were a clue that I just might be that combat-wounded Marine from South Carolina who was being considered for the Medal of Honor. I went out with some friends over the university's Parents Weekend, and we had trouble finishing our meal because families kept coming over asking to meet me. It was flattering but also a little confusing. I mean, I'm just a Marine who served like everyone else; I didn't understand why some people acted like they had spotted a celebrity. When we went to a Dave Matthews Band concert, I got bombarded by people wanting photos and asking questions. I tried to be as accommodating as possible, but it was also a little frustrating. It wasn't just that I was trying to enjoy the concert or the time with my friends, it was that people wanted to talk about my war experience, without stopping to consider that maybe I wasn't in the mood for that.

I think many veterans, especially ones with obvious injuries, face this struggle: We know people mean well, but sometimes we just want to be present in the moment rather than reliving difficult or painful memories from deployment. It's a difficult balance to strike, wanting to be gracious and accommodating while also protecting your own boundaries; this wasn't any kind of attention we ever asked for or even really wanted. And that day at the Dave Matthews Band concert, I was maxed out on being the guy people wanted me to be: Kyle Carpenter, War Hero. I was relieved when it was time to head home.

As we drew close to the exit, yet another group of people approached me and asked, "Will you take a picture of us?"

I forced a smile and said I would be happy to, but inside I was just exhausted from it all. I started walking over to them to put my arms around their shoulders, when the guy handed me his phone and said, with a confused look on his face, "No, we'd like you to take a picture *of* us, not *with* us."

Preston, who was with me, said he had never seen

someone so excited to grab a camera and start snapping photos in all his life. I took a dozen photos from different angles, trying to get the best shot of the stage, trying to avoid the sun behind them, trying to make sure everyone was smiling and no one had their eyes closed. I was so, so happy in that moment to just be a normal guy whom some people chose at random to take pictures. They probably thought it was pretty weird that the guy behind the camera was smiling even bigger than the people in front of it.

There have even been a few times when people weren't quite so gracious about wanting photos or talking to me about my injuries. As well, I've been criticized for posting photos from visits to the Middle East by people who think it's somehow wrong for me to want to visit a Muslim country or who seem upset that I'm not willing to condemn all Afghan people as terrorists.

One night, I was out with friends when this guy started running his mouth about how terrible it was that I was out at a bar instead of somehow polishing my legacy. I'm not sure what his problem with me was, but he seemed to take personal offense at the fact that I was out enjoying a rare evening away from the library. He seemed to think I had violated some code by having a beer out in town instead of standing up on a pedestal behind glass in my dress blues. He was itching for a fight, and I kept trying to ignore his remarks. Finally, I turned around and said, "I'm just trying to live my life, man."

I think that gets to the heart of what a lot of veterans feel: We are just trying to live our lives. We come back from deployment and try to move on and do what normal young men and women do: go to college, begin a career, start a family. We have lives outside our service records and find meaning beyond our time in the military, but some people seem to want to keep us in that one single role—for good or for bad—forever. I realize that veterans of Iraq and Afghanistan have it a whole lot better than vets from Vietnam did; the general tide of public opinion now is to support the troops even if you don't support the war. But it's still a challenge when people want to equate time in the military with sainthood. We're real people leading real lives. It is true that our experiences in the service are an indelible part of who we are, but that doesn't make us heroes, demons, saints, or cartoon characters. It makes us people with a certain set of life experiences.

I started to crave anonymity, even if just for a few days. I found that travel was a means to achieve it, and one of my favorite opportunities was when I was invited to visit a friend's family in Michoacán, Mexico.

I remember closing my eyes as I leaned back and listened to the sound of the gravel crunch beneath the tires of the old pickup truck. Sitting in a foldable chair placed in the bed of the truck, I swayed with every bump we hit on the dirt road as we wound our way through the mango fields and mountains, off the grid and deep in the heart of the country.

I had started out the day milking cows (which is much harder than you might think), and I had ended it pulling coconuts off trees. It's safe to say I was getting the local treatment. We made it back to the house just as the sun was setting behind the beautiful mountains that surrounded us. The deep shades of the orange and yellow sunset saturated the lush green palm-tree-covered land. It was one of those rare times that real life actually looked like a postcard. After the long day, I welcomed thoughts of dinner and sitting in the hammock with a fresh coconut with a straw in it for dessert afterward. So we unloaded the heavy bushels of coconuts from the truck and went inside to wash up.

My buddy told me the place we were going for dinner was a couple of houses down. I was confused because I hadn't met any neighbors or seen any restaurants nearby, but when we walked to the neighbors' home, there were tables and chairs that had been placed in the dirt road as people, stray dogs, and motorcycles worked their way around us. I learned that when the workday was over, two old ladies turned their front porch and kitchen into a small neighborhood restaurant. Everything came straight from the field that day and was made from scratch—and it was one of the best meals I have ever had in my life.

When it was time for the bill, we found that the four huge meals had cost a whopping eight dollars, and I needed to leave my Coke bottle so it could be recycled. I was humbled and amazed that, after working long, hard hours all day, these elderly women cooked into the night so they could make two dollars a meal to help support their families. I often think about them and the incredible food they prepared, and smile as I hope they are doing well.

As I traveled more, I cherished the stories of everyday people. From the villages of Afghanistan to tiny towns in central Mexico, the earth is full of people working hard to create a quiet, peaceful life for themselves. Most of us in comfortable, middle-class America will never know or appreciate how starkly different our way of life is—and how much beauty there is in so many ways of living. I wanted to learn how better to grasp the endless perspectives and experiences that can shape people, their unique worldviews, and our universal goals of making our own corners of the globe a little bit better with dignity and pride.

I also discovered that a bit of recognition can actually be really nice, not because it celebrates me but because it allows me to celebrate *with* the incredible people who are now part of my life.

On the afternoon of December 18, 2017, I was sitting in a folding chair on the floor of the Colonial Life Arena, adjusting my tassel to make sure it was positioned correctly on my cap. I was about to receive my diploma, making good on the promise I'd made myself and my parents eight years earlier that I'd one day go back to school and earn my degree. This time, college hadn't been a chore or a roadblock to my goals—it was both a stepping-stone to the next thing and a chapter in my life to be experienced for its own sake. My life before college had shaped me into the man I now was, with a sense of purpose and pride in both what I had already done and what I still had ahead of me to accomplish. Every phase of our lives builds on the next, and never was this more apparent than when the graduation speaker introduced me to the crowd and announced, "Joining Kyle's family this afternoon are members of his medical evacuation team and two of his doctors from Walter Reed National Military Medical Center.

Our thanks to you, Kyle. Would you please stand and receive our recognition?"

I stood . . . and suddenly, so did the entire arena. My fellow students were cheering, the crowd was cheering, my family was cheering. And I realized that I had really done it—we had really done it. My family, my peers, and all the people who'd kept me alive along the way—both literally and figuratively.

As I rebuilt my life, I learned that a lot of us fail to recognize the value and wisdom of our own unique set of experiences—the individual perspective that only we can offer. I think this becomes a particular challenge for anyone trying to start a second career or new phase in life. Even if we have deviated from the "traditional" path, we have inherent worth and a voice worth sharing. If the road that brought you to where you are now looks vastly different from everyone else's, that means you have more of a responsibility to speak up and share your perspective, not less. Even though I came to college with a completely different background than most of my classmates, it quickly became apparent how valuable my perspective was in helping me to define myself and build on the foundation it provided to create a meaningful life. I got so much more from my college experience coming at it the second time than I would have the first because of who I had become in the intervening years. That is one of the most worthwhile lessons I learned alongside my academic studies: Everything we've done in the past is a part of who we are now, but we are the only ones who get to choose who we become.

Chapter 16
You're Going to Fail . . .
and That's Okay

If you ever get blown up by a grenade, I do not advise running a marathon three months after getting out of the hospital.

But that's exactly what I planned to do in the fall of 2013, not long after I left Walter Reed. I started feeling so much better about my recovery and conditioning that I decided, at the beginning of October, that it would be a really good idea to try to run the Marine Corps Marathon at the end of the month, with just a few weeks of actual training. The marathon route twists through Washington, D.C., and ends at the Marine Corps War Memorial (more commonly known as the Iwo Jima statue) in Arlington, Virginia. In other words, it was basically in my backyard while I was at the hospital. What better motivator for me to push myself toward even greater recovery goals than to attempt a marathon? And since it was so close, what excuse did I have not to? (I mean, aside from the whole grenade thing, of course.)

Before I got injured, the idea of running a marathon had always been a vague bucket list item. But now that I had actually died—twice—and a marathon was somehow still possible, I knew I had to do it. I was not that far removed from just being able to sit up with my legs over the edge of the bed for five minutes at a time and needing a team of six people to help me go to the bathroom. Running the marathon would be proof that I was back, and even better and stronger than before.

Despite my lack of preparation, that 2013 marathon was absolutely incredible. I shocked myself by completing it in 4:27, and crossing the finish line was one of the greatest feelings of my life. It was a good thing I had sunglasses on because I teared up at the end. I had just unexpectedly inspired myself: I couldn't believe that I had survived my injury, and if I hadn't survived, I would have never had this or any of the other amazing experiences I had had over the past three years.

I definitely paid for it afterward, though. We conveniently forget that the original marathoner back in ancient Greece, Pheidippides, dropped dead at the end of his run, and my body felt like that might have been a better option. It wasn't just that my muscles were still fighting back from being atrophied, it was also that my lungs had not been put through that kind of a workout and my heart hadn't been pushed to do that much work in close to a year. Running a marathon was a far cry from doing thirty leisurely minutes on the machines in physical therapy as a cooldown. I limped straight from the finish line to my hotel to shower and catch the next flight back to South Carolina because I had a midterm exam at eight-thirty the following morning. As I limped through a painful post-race recovery for about a week, I took solace in the fact that I had now done the major-life-event-followed-by-a-marathon thing, and I'd never have to do it again. It was, I told myself, a once-in-a-lifetime experience.

After all, there were lots of other adventures on that bucket list. I'd always been an adrenaline junkie, and it was proving to be a lot of fun to let that side of me loose after all of my time in the hospital. The year after my first marathon, I got the chance to one-up myself by skydiving with Team Fastrax ("America's Sky Diving Team") onto the starting line of the 2014 Marine Corps Marathon. Two jumpers would leap out holding a massive American flag, and the rest of us would follow in formation. Then I would run the race! How could I possibly say no to that?

Mom and Dad were of course concerned and, predictably, came up with plenty of ways I could say no, but the opportunity was too awesome to decline. "I'm going to make you start paying for my hair dye to cover all of the gray you give me," my mom would insist every time another wild opportunity came up, and this time was no exception. But nothing she said or did was going to stop me.

I forgot to account for a different mother: Mother Nature.

It was a particularly windy October morning as we took off, but all of the jumpers on the team were experienced, mostly retired Special Forces members, and knew how to compensate for the weather, so I wasn't concerned. What I didn't realize, however, is that you can only compensate so much; wind patterns are too unpredictable to completely overcome. Our plane circled over the Pentagon, waiting for exactly the right moment after the sun broke the horizon before we jumped. Unfortunately, I wore out my legs squatting for half an hour as we waited for our cue. Even more unfortunate, we were blown pretty significantly off course, and missed the startling line by a lot. From where the runners and spectators were gathered, all they could see was the jump team falling and then me and one other jumper disappearing behind some tall trees in the distance. My mom had insisted on showing up for the race, just in case I died jumping, and the last thing she saw was me falling out of the sky and potentially crash-landing in Arlington National Cemetery.

From my point of view, it was a less-than-ideal start to the race. I had to drop my gear and sprint toward the line, weaving in and out of headstones, as the starting gun was raised in the air a long, long way in the distance. I honestly don't even know how far I had to run just to get to the starting line, but beginning a race with exhausted legs was hardly a setup for my best time. So with that in mind, I was pretty proud of my 5:12. I completed the same post-race routine as 2013: finish line to hotel to shower to airport to class the next morning.

I will never forget when I stumbled into class the next day, though. My political science professor kept giving me confused looks when I arrived at his ten-thirty class; finally, he came up to me after the lecture and admitted he followed me on Instagram. "Um . . . did you run a marathon in Washington, D.C., yesterday?" he asked.

I laughed and said yes. He seemed impressed, and definitely believed me when he saw how long it took me to stand up and walk out of the classroom.

That experience in 2014 made me hungry for a third try. So after toying with the idea for a couple of years, I set my sights on 2017. I was determined to dominate that third marathon. Sub–four hours—that was my goal. No more of this decide-to-train-four-weeks-ahead-of-time nonsense. No dramatic arrival. No, I would enter that third marathon with an athlete's mind-set. I was going to train hard, eat well, and crush the 26.2 miles that lay ahead of me. After all, I had spent the last seven years overcoming any obstacle in my path. I thought back to my pre-deployment mind-set in 2010, and how naive I was to believe I was invincible then. I hadn't been through anything at that point to warrant such tremendous confidence in myself. But now? Now was a different story. I had survived the unsurvivable. Nothing could stop me.

I trained religiously for months, and I felt completely confident and relaxed on race day. The gun fired and I set off, feeling great and enjoying the weather, warmer than on my previous two marathons. Unfortunately, the temperature continued to rise until it was way hotter than usual. Still, I was cruising at just under a four-hour pace when I reached mile eighteen, and I was sure that this was going to be my year to top my personal best. Then the cramping started. No matter how much water I grabbed, how many GU packs I ate as I ran, it wasn't enough to beat back the knots in my muscles. They started in my calves and worked their way up through my thighs and even crept into the muscles on the sides of my hips. First, I had to swallow my pride and walk a little; then I had to start staggering, stiff-legged, like the Tin Man, because I couldn't even bend my knees.

Finally, at mile twenty-two I dragged myself over to the side of the road and started vomiting. Muscles I didn't even know I had began locking up. I kept trying to convince myself that I could keep going and I'd be able to pick right back up and finish the last four miles, but I couldn't move. To make matters worse, this happened just yards away from a medical tent. While that might actually sound like good news, it was the worst possible scenario I could have imagined because the staff saw what was happening and pulled me into the tent for evaluation, officially crushing any of the dwindling hope I had for making my goal time. As I sat there in the tent, dying to get the all-clear to get back on the course, the staff did bloodwork, checked my electrolytes, and confirmed I was not on the verge of a seizure—all while pumping me full of Gatorade and water. Finally, when I asked if I could return to my run, I ended up in a twenty-minute argument with the medical staff, mainly a wonderful Navy doctor, Dr.

O'Connor, who kept advising me that it wasn't worth it to risk a heat stroke or worse just to try to finish the last four miles. Eventually, I was able to wear them down and they agreed to release me after I signed a waiver acknowledging that they had advised, and then *strongly* advised, that I not complete the race.

Was it a dumb decision? Absolutely. The medical staff were right—there was absolutely no way I should have been allowed back onto the course. But I knew that if I didn't complete the last four miles, I would never forgive myself. I was already angry I hadn't made my time; I wasn't going to be talked into quitting altogether. Up until now, I hadn't ever really hit a wall with my physical training. Sure, I had encountered limitations, but I was always able to push past any obstacle through mental tenacity. The more success I enjoyed, the more ambitious my goals became. For the first time in a while, I was reminded that the best-laid plans don't always work out. It was a lesson I needed to learn, but I didn't want a medical tent at mile twenty-two of a marathon to be the place where I finally accepted the fact that I'm not Superman. I figured that even if I couldn't finish the race, at least I'd know I had tried. Once you make the choice to continue, it's easier to make it again. I thought of my bleeding blisters during the Crucible at boot camp. I had every medical reason in the world to throw in the towel and no one would have faulted me. But I had to keep going.

I left the medical tent and did a weird half-walk, half-jog, stiff-legged stumble to the finish line. Every step had me asking myself, *Am I going to be able to do this?* And the answer was, honestly, for the first time in my life: *Probably not.* I mean, what was I doing it for at that point? To prove I could? I'd already done it twice before with better times; this really didn't matter. Bragging rights? I'd survived a grenade explosion; I hoped I had at least *some* bragging rights locked down for life. There was absolutely no reason in the world to continue . . . except that I knew that it would affect the way I carried myself afterward. And so I did.

That marathon taught me an invaluable lesson on the importance of accepting failure. After my injury, I needed every win that came my way. It was vital that I be able to see myself as someone who was unstoppable, no matter the circumstances. That was the mind-set I needed to help carry me through the toughest days of therapy, the never-ending surgeries, and the mind-numbing rehab—to reassert my own power and independence. All those little successes empowered me to believe that my progress was not a fluke and my healing wasn't accidental or temporary; it was earned. And because I am naturally stubborn, I was pretty relentless until I was able to achieve what I was aiming for, every single time. But now I'd started to believe that maybe I really was invincible.

Of course, I wasn't. When I finally dragged myself across the 2017 Marine Corps Marathon finish line at just over six hours, I was angry, frustrated, and humbled. And that was exactly what I needed. I needed to be reminded that the outcome didn't really matter; the force that was driving me to keep pushing—and even to attempt such an ambitious goal in the first place—was really the most important thing. Trying and failing was a disappointment; never trying at all would have been a huge disappointment.

There is a quote from Teddy Roosevelt that sums up this idea perfectly: "The credit belongs to the man who is actually in the arena; whose face is marred by the dust and sweat and blood; who strives valiantly . . . who, at worst, if he fails, at least fails while daring greatly; so that his place shall never be with those cold and timid souls who know neither victory nor defeat." It is the act of striving that marks the difference between true success and failure. All of my exhaustive preparing, all of my long, intense training—none of it had mattered in the end. I failed. But what did matter was that I put one painful foot in front of the other.

Sometimes, we don't get what we plan for. Sometimes, everything can go wrong even when you do everything right. You're going to fail . . . and that's okay. The question is what you do with that knowledge. If you don't even try because you *might* miss your goal, you miss out on life. We are all going to face defeat, and more than just once or twice. How you react under those circumstances is what matters—do you give up? Do you push on? Do you give it your best shot for your own peace of mind even when you know it's a lost cause?

That, to me, is the real measure of perseverance; it not only shows us who we are but also forces us to think about what we could become.

Chapter 17
You Are More Than
Your Ribbon Rack or Résumé

Throughout 2013, buzz began to grow around the Medal of Honor investigation. The *Marine Corps Times* ran a series of articles about it, as did a number of other news outlets. If my actions during the grenade attack were deemed worthy of the medal, I would become the youngest living Medal of Honor recipient and only the second living Marine recipient since the Vietnam War—a fact that seemed to intrigue a lot of reporters.

I was aware of the interest, but I never really dwelled on it. I was still convinced nothing was going to come of it. And I was so consumed with school and my growing speaking career—which had started small, with school groups and local civic organizations around Columbia, but pretty quickly expanded to corporate settings and then to even larger venues—that I didn't have time to think about much else. And it wasn't really something I was seeking, anyway.

This last point is hard to explain to people who haven't had combat experience. Nobody goes into a battle with the goal of receiving a medal for valor, much less the Medal of Honor. No one hopes that their squad or their buddies end up in such a perilous situation that trying to save lives becomes necessary. The Medal of Honor is not something people seek, plain and simple.

The previous November, in 2013, I had gotten a call from Major Kendra Motz, a public affairs officer at Headquarters Marine Corps in Washington, D.C. Even though the investigation was not complete, she felt it was important to begin working with me now on how to handle the media attention that comes with being considered for the Medal of Honor. Since I was already headed to D.C. for the Commandant's Marine Corps Birthday Ball, I told her we could meet while I was in town.

At first, we went over some of the basics regarding how to prepare for increased notoriety and how to protect my privacy—the sort of things that come with celebrity. Several people at the Pentagon had told me I might want to change my Twitter handle, as it could be seen as unprofessional or irreverent. So I made a point of asking Major Motz when we got to the social media discussion, "What do you think of my social media handle? Do you think I should keep it or change it? It's @chiksdigscars."

It may sound like a small issue in the grand scheme of things, but it was an important intersection for me mentally. I had thought about it for a long time. If I changed who I was, even in a small way, before any of this even began, if it began—where might that lead? I was prepared to dig in my heels and defend it as funny and harmless.

Thankfully, she laughed. "It's hilarious. Keep it."

Throughout the winter we kept talking, but I still didn't say much about the investigation to anyone besides my family and a couple of close and trusted friends. The Medal of Honor decision is supposed to be kept quiet until there is an official announcement and I couldn't quite wrap my head around it. My parents were great about making sure I wasn't taking on too much, and Paul offered his helpful perspective as an active-duty Marine. Together they helped me figure out how to navigate the unusual situation of being medically retired and a full-time student, but still having a foot in the military world as a candidate for such an incredible honor—and not being able to tell anyone about it.

One afternoon when I had miraculously gotten ahead on my coursework and didn't have anywhere to be other than our apartment, Preston and I were watching *The Dark Knight Rises* while I played on my phone. Out of nowhere, I suddenly remarked, "You know, I'm being considered for the Medal of Honor." I don't know why I chose that moment to share the news, but I had been turning the matter over and over in my head and I figured he should probably be aware so it didn't take him by surprise if it did happen. He looked over at me from the other sofa and just blinked. "Are . . . are you . . . serious?" he stammered.

"Yeah. There's an investigation going on into the event."

"Dude, that's amazing! I'm so excited for you!"

"Thanks, man," I said, and that was about it. I think Preston understood that since I didn't even know what was going on, I probably wasn't ready to talk about it, but he also knew that life might be about to get really different for me, and as my roommate and one of my best friends, it could impact him. Really, though, I think I just needed to practice saying it out loud and gauging the response from someone who didn't know anything about it. Like I said, there had been discussion about the possibility in the media, but most college students did not follow that sort of thing closely. If the medal really was going to be awarded—and my protocol team seemed to think it would—I was going to have to be comfortable with the idea of it, and that meant at least being able to talk about it matter-of-factly.

The calendar turned over to 2014, and I continued to work with Major Motz, Gunnery Sergeant Chanin Nuntavong, and the rest of the protocol team, even though there was still no word on whether the medal was going forward or not. I figured that whichever conclusion the Marine Corps came to, at least I would know that every detail of that day I can't remember would be thoroughly researched and vetted.

Then, finally, on an unassuming day in February, I was notified that I should expect a call from President Obama the following Monday at 1:36 P.M. This seemed weirdly specific, until I remembered that the leader of the free world has more than a few demands on his time and probably runs a pretty tight schedule. I told my parents, of course, but they didn't say a word of it to my brothers; I think we thought it would be more fun for them to be caught off guard.

The day of the call, I had class in the morning, then drove home (about thirty miles), since I wanted to receive the phone call with my family. Meanwhile, my dad had picked up Peyton from Lexington High

School. Price was attending King Academy and had driven himself to school, so Mom called the headmaster and asked that Price be released to come home. When they were both there, Mom and Dad told them that there was going to be a surprise and asked if they had any guesses.

"Is it a new dog?" one of them asked.

"Is Dad getting a new recliner?" the other one guessed.

"What in the world?" my mom demanded while my dad cracked up. "Do you honestly think we would take you out of school just because your father replaced his junky old chair?"

My mom's complete bewilderment at her sons continued when I walked in the door a few minutes later and my first words were: "Does anyone have a phone charger? I'm at seven percent."

"Are you kidding me? . . . Kyle, are you serious?" my mom roared. "The president is about to call you and your phone isn't even charged?" She also seemed a little distressed by the fact that I was wearing a gray hoodie over a green T-shirt and some comfortable old leather shoes she called "nasty." It wasn't a video call so I didn't understand why she was so confounded by my wardrobe choice, but she found me a cord and I was successfully plugged in and charging by 1:30—which is a good thing, because the call came through at 1:36 on the dot.

I remember being surprised that an actual number appeared on my phone screen, rather than an "unknown caller" message, but it must have been the number for the central switchboard for the White House. I answered the phone, and a stern-sounding woman on the other end announced: "Stand by, I have the President of the United States on the phone for you."

"Okay" was all I could get out after such a profound statement. A moment later, a voice familiar to me came on.

"Kyle?!" said the president in a surprisingly conversational, friendly, and upbeat tone. It immediately set me at ease . . . or as much at ease as you can be when you're talking to the Commander in Chief.

"Yes, sir?"

"How ya doin'?"

"I'm fine, sir. How are you?"

Am I really making small talk with the president?

"I'm doing just fine, thanks!" he answered. Then he continued: "It's my pleasure to let you know that based on the recommendation of the Secretary of the Navy and the Secretary of Defense, I have approved the Medal of Honor to be awarded to you for your courageous actions in Afghanistan in support of Operation Enduring Freedom."

There it was. It was happening. I hadn't really believed it—not when I got the first call in Guapo's two years earlier, not when Dr. Daso talked about it, not when Major Motz started working with me, not even when I was told to expect a call from the president. Not until I heard the words from President Obama himself. Despite all the preparation for that moment, it still caught me by surprise.

The president spoke a little more, telling me how proud he was of the job I and my fellow Marines had done. He added, "Thank you from my family and the nation." I thanked him as well, and then the call ended. My mom was crying, my dad was proudly smiling at me, my brothers were absolutely dumbfounded—and hopefully not too disappointed we didn't get that new recliner! Sadie was running around checking on all her people, sensing that something big had just happened and wanting to make sure we were all okay. We had a few minutes as a family, just reflecting on what a journey the last three and a half years had been for us.

Then it was time for me to get back in my car and drive to campus for my afternoon classes. It was a little surreal to be on the phone with the president and then to be walking into a classroom half an hour later, but it was also a perfect reminder that my life would never be defined by the medal.

It was a tough decision but I ended up withdrawing from school that semester due to the amount of preparation required ahead of the Medal of Honor ceremony and the time I would have to dedicate afterward for interviews and media tours. I hated not finishing the term, but I have always believed in at least trying to be all in wherever I am and whatever I'm doing. I knew that this needed my entire attention. The crazy thing was, even though my family knew, the official announcement was not slated to go out until May, with the ceremony taking place at the White House a month after that. In other words, I had to keep the news quiet for three months.

I made several trips to the Pentagon, where I did mock interviews with Major Motz and her team to practice being on camera. These weren't simply Q-and-A sessions; they were intense, hours-long interrogations where I was getting drilled with every crazy, hostile, or uncomfortably prying question someone might try to throw at me. I learned how to shut down any inquiry I wasn't comfortable with and instead to steer the conversation in a better direction. Then I had to study up on protocol for the White House ceremony and figure out how to trim the enormous pool of people who had shown me love and support to a guest list of one hundred. Mom and I agonized over that list; it almost would have been easier if I could only have invited ten. I worked really hard to pull from all the different spheres of my life to represent a full picture of my experience. Besides my family, of course, I wanted my buddies from 2/9, since this award was as much a part of their experience as mine; I wanted my doctors, surgeons, and therapists there so they could be publicly recognized for the incredible work they did; I wanted people who had served as professional mentors for me along the way, from my old drill instructors Luke Billingsley and Anthony Richard to Paul Ramirez to Dr. Daso from my military history class. It was a difficult list to make, and I wasn't sure how many people were actually going to come, but I did my best to honor everyone who had made me the person I was leading up to the grenade attack, as well as the ones who had shaped my life afterward.

In April, the Marine Corps sent a Combat Camera crew out to my parents' house to film for several days. Combat Camera is a team that documents noteworthy events in the Marine Corps for information, education, morale, and archiving purposes. Their goal was to create a series of short films about various aspects of my service: my letters home, my deployment and injury, my recovery, and so forth. It was strange having a camera following me around like I was on a reality TV show, but the men and women on the crew were nice and did their best to be invisible when filming so that my family and I could act as natural as possible.

Then, on May 19, 2014, the White House issued the official announcement, with the ceremony set for June 19.

Wednesday, June 18, dawned hot and muggy, just like every summer day in D.C. I was excited, but also a little nervous to see my friends as they started to arrive at the hotel. My Marine buddies Jared, Scott, Mike, Griffin, and Dominic Davila arrived one by one from wherever they were stationed or living at the time, and it was the most incredible reunion. I was excited to introduce Paul to the guys who hadn't met him yet, since he had been such a significant mentor for me at Walter Reed. We had a little reception at the hotel that night, where we shared stories and laughed about the kinds of crazy antics that only happen on deployment or in the barracks when you're young, dumb, and bored. I don't know when I have ever laughed so hard in my life.

Afterward, my friends went out to enjoy the evening in D.C., but I opted to go to bed early since I had the next day's ceremony weighing on my mind. I went over my uniform about a thousand times to make sure everything was absolutely perfect, then struggled to get to sleep before waking up early to go back over it a thousand times more. I only remember two things before leaving the hotel for the White House. The first was that I was interrupted from a daze by Gunnery Sergeant Nuntavong, telling me it was time to get dressed. I had been standing in front of the window of my hotel room, staring down at D.C., woven with national monuments and the rolling hills of white headstones at Arlington Cemetery, and wondering if all of this was really happening. The second thing I remember is, after getting dressed, all of my closest friends and loved ones came by my room to give me a hug and tell me they loved me.

Finally, right after an early lunch, I put on my dress blues. (As an interesting side note, officers have a summer dress blue uniform that has white trousers instead of blue ones, but an enlisted Marine can only wear white trousers in extremely limited circumstances—one of which is meeting with the Commander in Chief. Which I was. So I had a new pair of white trousers I was probably only going to wear once.) Per my official instructions, I reported with my family to the Executive Avenue entrance to the White House thirty minutes before the start time. Even though we were on a tight schedule, I had to take a couple of minutes to pet the Obamas' dogs, Bo and Sunny, who were hanging out with the Secret Service in their small security checkpoint building. After playtime, I was ushered into the East Room, where the protocol team talked through the order of the ceremony quickly so I could have a feel for how things would go; I also practiced standing on the tape marks that indicated precisely the right angle for me to turn for the president to put the medal around my neck. Then I was introduced to the president and first lady in the Oval Office, where we talked for a few minutes before he signed the Medal of Honor citation and certificate with me standing beside his desk. At that point, it was time for the ceremony to begin, so I walked with the Obamas through the Blue Room back to the East Room, where a huge crowd of special guests, dignitaries, members of the Medal of Honor Society (past recipients), journalists, photographers and camera crews, and my invitees were assembled.

A couple of things happened in that ceremony that have apparently never happened before. After the opening prayer, President Obama greeted the crowd and said, "The man you see before you today should not be alive today. Hand grenades are one of the most awful weapons of war." Then, despite all of the rehearsals and going over what I was and was not supposed to do, I completely forgot to stand still during the president's remarks. I think it's important to look at people, most especially the president, when they speak to you, and the way the tape mark was positioned, I almost had my back to him. It felt a little disrespectful, and since no one had told me I couldn't, I broke my position of attention so I could turn and see him. The cameras went crazy; it sounded like a huge flock of birds swooped into the room. Then, instead of standing at attention and maintaining a poker face, I smiled and laughed a little after he pointed out in his speech that I don't hide my scars: "He tells me this—so I'm just quoting him—but he says the girls definitely like them. So he's working an angle on this thing." I had no idea he was going to share that so it caught me off guard, and the president's delivery was perfect. Also, President Obama actually got choked up while reading about my recovery, which I've been told was a first; normally, the president does not show emotion to that extent. But the final break in protocol was one that was actually approved, and that was having my medical care team stand to be recognized. I had asked the White House planning committee ahead of time if we could give them special recognition for their unbelievable work, and everyone agreed that it would be appropriate. None of my doctors or therapists had any idea that was coming, so it was special for me and every person in the world watching to be able to witness their surprise as the president asked them to stand and the room erupted in well-deserved applause.

After President Obama concluded his remarks, a naval officer and military White House aide read the citation while a Marine aide held the medal:

For conspicuous gallantry and intrepidity at the risk of his life above and beyond the call of duty while serving as an Automatic Rifleman with Company F, 2nd Battalion, 9th Marines, Regimental Combat Team 1, 1st Marine Division (Forward), 1 Marine Expeditionary Force (Forward), in Helmand Province, Afghanistan in support of Operation Enduring Freedom on 21 November 2010. Lance Corporal Carpenter was a member of a platoon-sized coalition force, comprised of two reinforced Marine squads, partnered with an Afghan National Army squad. The platoon had established Patrol Base Dakota two days earlier in a small village in the Marjah District in order to disrupt enemy activity and provide security for the local Afghan population. Lance Corporal Carpenter and a fellow Marine were manning a rooftop security position on the perimeter of Patrol Base Dakota when the enemy initiated a daylight attack with hand grenades, one of which landed inside their sandbagged position. Without hesitation and with complete disregard for his own safety, Lance Corporal Carpenter moved towards the grenade in an attempt to shield his fellow Marine from the deadly blast. When the grenade detonated, his body absorbed the brunt of the blast, severely wounding him but saving the life of his fellow Marine. By his undaunted courage, bold fighting spirit, and unwavering devotion to duty in the face of almost certain death, Lance Corporal Carpenter reflected great credit upon himself and upheld the highest traditions of the Marine Corps and the United States Naval Service.

Then the president placed the medal around my neck and shook my hand, and the audience clapped before the ceremony closed with a prayer. He invited everyone to stay for the reception ("I understand that the food here at the White House is pretty good so I already told Kyle's brothers that they should be chowing down. But that goes for everyone else as well.") and then he took a few minutes to talk with the Marines I had served with who were in attendance. I was so glad that they had a chance to meet our Commander in Chief as well.

After everything wrapped up, I called Major Motz over in an urgent whisper. She shot me an inquisitive look and said, "What's wrong?"

I felt a little panicked. As a Marine, I knew my uniform should be absolutely perfect. I pointed to the medal, which was hanging off-kilter. "Can you fix this? I don't think it's supposed to look like this but I don't want to correct the president."

She rolled her eyes at me and laughed, "Oh, jeez— come here, Kyle." And she straightened it out so it laid properly on my uniform. I breathed a little easier after that. Dr. Daso pointed out to me later that when the medal was slightly off-center, it was actually lying on my Purple Heart.

An unfortunate truth I learned is that everything at the White House begins and ends on time—even if it's a party that's being given in your honor, and even if you are late to it because you were talking to the president. After the behind-the-scenes chatting with President Obama, I went out to the reception . . . where the food was already being packed up and the party was over. I was extremely hungry and was able to snag two little prime rib sliders that were the most beautiful, perfectly cut sandwiches I'd ever seen in my life—and that was it. I could have eaten an MRE off the floor I was so hungry, but all I got was a teasing sample of what I had missed as it was whisked away. (If anyone who works in the White House kitchen is reading this, I want a rain check someday!)

Following the reception, we went back to the hotel for an hour or two, then we were scheduled for a dinner at the National Museum of the Marine Corps at Quantico that evening. We loaded on a bus, and I-95 was shut down to accommodate our motorcade on the thirty-five-mile drive south. It was more than a little amazing to me to realize that the same interstate my mother and I had driven from South Carolina to D.C. during those six months I was recovering at home was now shut down—for me! Never in a million years would I have guessed at that time where that journey would lead.

As we made our way through northern Virginia, I marveled at the wide-open interstate and police escort we had. There was a guy who started nosing his way onto the highway as we passed; I'm not sure if he just wasn't paying attention or was really late for an appointment or what, but he kept trying to drive past the motorcycle cop who had stopped traffic on the on-ramp. That officer was having none of it, and as the car made one more attempt to sneak past him, the cop sputtered over on his bike and gave it some kind of Spartan war-kick right in the side fender to make him stop. It worked. I felt bad for the driver, but that ninja cop was pretty awesome to watch.

The following day, I was presented with my official Medal of Honor flag at a ceremony hosted by the Commandant and Sergeant Major of the Marine Corps at the famous Marine barracks and parade ground at 8th and I Streets, "the oldest post in the Corps," and strategically placed within running distance of the U.S. Capitol building in case of an attack. It was established by President Thomas Jefferson in 1801. That afternoon, after remarks from Secretary of Defense Chuck Hagel, I was inducted into the Hall of Heroes at the Pentagon.

The next two weeks were sort of a whirlwind of TV and public appearances: interviews on *Fox & Friends* and *Morning Joe*, throwing out the first pitch for the San Diego Padres, and, of course, an appearance on the *Late Show with David Letterman*. I even got to ring the opening bell on the Wall Street trading floor. Every night I sat down with Major Motz and Gunny Nuntavong to go over notes from that day and to prepare for the next one. I had a sleep block designated from midnight to 5:00 A.M., but I usually didn't get to bed until around two, because we had to prep my uniform for the next day. The media tour was exhausting, but a vital part of receiving the medal: You tell your story, which in turn helps to tell the story of the entire military. It allows American citizens to have a different look at the people and experiences that make up the military, and it helps humanize and put a face on our nation's overseas operations.

As great as those discussions were and as wonderful as everyone was on each of those programs, it could be challenging; I didn't ever want anyone to think that the significance of the medal was being reduced to entertainment.

The thing I want people to understand is that the Medal of Honor is a heavy distinction. It only weighs a couple of ounces, but the physical weight is nothing compared to the weight of what it represents. Everything that medal symbolizes—not just the circumstances under which it was earned, but the broader conflict of which that action was a part and all of the losses that are a result of that conflict—adds weight.

One of my friends from deployment told me that when he saw the president place the medal around my neck, he cried, because "our unit, our story, and the guys we lost will never die after that." For my fellow Marines, he said, the medal was a part of everyone's deployment. I understood exactly what he meant. You go out on each patrol with no clue as to what you will encounter—maybe it's completely uneventful or maybe you end up in an hours-long firefight. If the latter, you have to come back to base and document how far away the enemy was, how long the fight lasted, what firepower was used, what casualties there were. Then you get a ribbon for your uniform that says you were in combat and someone shot at you. And if someone puts you in for a commendation medal, which is a step above that, and says, "Hey—you did a really good job," *that* award has to collect all sorts of signatures and might take months to get approved and, meanwhile, you've had a dozen more experiences just as harrowing. In other words, no one's ribbon rack ever tells the full story of their service. But having served alongside someone who was awarded the Medal of Honor somehow helps to capture in a bigger sense what we all went through.

Even beyond our current operations, when you start trying to add up each casualty, each death, each injury, the mental scars, and every person listed as MIA over nearly 250 years of military conflicts—it's overwhelming.

I marvel, too, at all the tremendous acts of bravery and heroism—from the Civil War, Spanish American War, WWI, WWII, Korea, Vietnam, Desert Storm, Somalia, OEF, OIF, even to the Special Forces and intelligence communities, who operate without recognition in places we will never know—that never got told. Maybe those stories weren't told because there was no one around to witness them. Maybe they weren't told because no one survived to tell them. Maybe they *were* told, but some external factor stood in the way of someone getting the honor they deserved. That's why I often say the medal doesn't belong to me—not really. My story just happened to be noticed. Thinking of the Medal of Honor as an individual award couldn't be further from the truth.

I don't care what anybody says about why we are in Afghanistan or Iraq—whether the wars are just or unjust or politically motivated or driven by one set of beliefs or another. I know that war is hell. But it is also fought by some of the bravest, kindest, most remarkable human beings I will ever have the privilege of knowing. I've seen with my own eyes Marines take a knee in front of civilians during firefights, putting themselves between local kids and bad guys. I have seen our corpsmen and medics bandage the enemy because of injuries they sustained trying to get away on their motorcycle after shooting at us. Because, at the end of the day, the U.S. military is there to *protect and help.* Maybe some of the big-picture reasons as to why we are in a region may not make sense to everyone (sometimes not even to the men and women on the ground serving). But as a Marine, each night as you lay your head on your pillow, or on the dirt, and realize it could have been your last day on earth, there is satisfaction in knowing that you are there to help other human beings. The fact is that the men and women of our military better the lives of people around the globe every day, and that is something we should all be proud to say.

To me, the medal represents all of that—all of the lives given in pursuit of that idea. It represents every person who has taken up arms against true injustice. It stands as a beacon of hope for struggling, oppressed people around the world who will risk their lives to save one another. As someone who has been given that honor, knowing that my behavior and words and actions all reflect what the medal stands for, I want my decisions to make those who came before me and those who come after me proud. As I said, the medal may weigh only a couple ounces, but that is a heavier weight than I can put into words.

I am grateful for the honor—deeply, eternally grateful. And I am proud to be a bearer of the tradition and legacy. But that doesn't mean that I—or any of the recipients—are excited about it. It's not an Academy Award or a pageant title. It is not something we "won"—in fact, there are no Medal of Honor "winners," only Medal of Honor recipients. It's not a competition. It's not a prize we were vying for. It's a recognition of something that we did that most wish had never happened in the first place. I'm lucky; I can barely remember anything of the grenade explosion. For many other Medal of Honor recipients, that award invokes the worst memories of their life. And even those men are lucky, because they survived. After all, ever since the Medal of Honor was created during the Civil War, most have been awarded posthumously.

In fact, "my" Medal of Honor is not on display in my home. I don't know if the White House budget for award boxes was cut or what, but I never received a case for it. A few months after my ceremony, however, I noticed my GoPro case was about the right size, so that's where I keep it now, on a shelf in my closet in my apartment. If I am asked to speak to a veteran-heavy crowd, I will sometimes take the medal along and instead of wearing it, I will pass it around so that they can see it and read what's on the back and feel the history of the country through it, in a way. Even though the Medal of Honor privileges permit recipients to wear the medal with "appropriate" civilian clothes "at their pleasure," I never put on the medal unless I am asked to—and even then I only wear it if it is for an appropriate reason or cause. I won't put it on just because someone wants a photo or to raise money; it's not a prop. In fact, that's been one of the hardest things for me to learn to adjust to: being able to say no to people's requests. I've had event planners and corporate leaders ask multiple times with frustration why I won't put on my uniform and endorse their products or cause, but I just don't think some people understand what the medal really represents.

All told, I don't think I've worn the medal more than a dozen times since 2014.

Survivor's guilt is real. It doesn't matter what branch of the service you are in, the Marines, soldiers, sailors, and airmen alongside you feel like an extension of yourself because you're all in this together. If your truck rolled over an IED and you survived but the three guys with you in the truck didn't, what kind of burdens do you carry? If you're conducting a checkpoint and the female soldier next to you steps forward to conduct the pat down on the lady in a burqa who, it turns out, is hiding a suicide vest, how do you reconcile that? You blame yourself for not spotting the IED or the irregular folds in the fabric. You beat yourself up over not knowing then the things you only know now. You hear people try to reassure you—"It's not your fault"—and you know they mean well, but it doesn't change the fact that you made it home when someone else didn't. It doesn't erase from your mind the image of an empty chair at their family's table.

You try to focus on the silver linings: that your friend who was killed at nineteen from a mortar round or stepping on an IED was someone who raised their right hand to serve when they didn't have to. They will go down forever as a hero who died doing *something*, rather than passing into middle age, losing their hair, and looking back as they silently ask themselves *What if?* They will always be young and brave and with their last breath they spoke their name on the winds of history. Now your job, as someone who survived, is to honor their life by living your own to the fullest.

The only reason I'm comfortable saying this is because I thought I was going to be one of those guys who didn't make it back. I thought I was going to bleed out and be dead at twenty-one, then a month later I suddenly woke up to a bonus round—and that's awesome. But the weight of knowing you're here and someone else is not isn't something you can simply snap out of.

The loss of community is real, too. When you come back from deployment and the men and women who were in the trenches to the right and left of you get transferred across the country and other people get out of the service and people move back home—it leaves an empty feeling. Nothing will ever replace the camaraderie you had when your lives were on the line and you only had each other.

The Medal of Honor represents all of that and more. It is an awe-inspiring and humbling award that is heavy with history. It represents the unimaginable service and sacrifice of a very few, but we were all just doing what anyone else would have done in our position to save the people around us. We made one of the countless choices we make throughout our lives. And if we were lucky enough to survive, we then have an infinite number of new choices to make about how to live our lives moving forward.

Because the event that earned the medal was really just that—an event. A moment. A minuscule speck of time that has everything and nothing to do with what came before or after. We are caretakers of the medal for the next generation of warriors who will inherit its legacy and all it represents, for the people who came before us. I am more than my ribbon rack or résumé, and so are you. I wouldn't say that all my life was preparing me for that moment on the roof—more like that moment was part of the chain of events that was preparing me for life. A life of purpose. A life of service. A life of leading. A life worth fighting for. And a legacy worth protecting.

Chapter 18
Say Thank You

Robin Carpenter raised her sons to understand the importance of writing thank-you notes. Even before the wrapping paper had been gathered up at every Christmas or birthday, my brothers and I were sitting at the kitchen table, note cards and pencils in hand, whining our way through a series of thank-you notes to grandparents, aunts, uncles, and friends. Due to my parents' insistence on old-fashioned manners, I grew up with an inherent sense of appreciation. Teachers, bus drivers, lunch ladies, old folks at church, the bag boy at the grocery store—we were brought up to thank everyone, everywhere, as a matter of common courtesy.

Old habits die hard.

Imagine, then, the struggle of how adequately to thank the men and women who worked exhaustively to save my life and the countless people who were part of the effort to restore my body and independence over almost three years of hospitalization. I tried to capture a fraction of that appreciation by having my medical team recognized at the Medal of Honor ceremony. But how could I possibly thank the people who were my first responders as I made my way from Afghanistan to the United States? Besides Doc Frend, I didn't know their names and I certainly didn't remember their faces. How would I ever be able to show my appreciation for the people who lifted me from the rooftop, who brought me back to life—more than once—and who managed to stabilize me enough to get me home from Germany?

I struggled for a long time with the fact that I couldn't properly thank all of the extraordinary people who went to extraordinary lengths to care for me, comfort me, and help me in a hundred different capacities. I had received so much from them without being able to offer them anything in return, even just an acknowledgment of what they did for me. That guilt was persistent. True, I spent four years mentally and physically worn down from learning to live again, swimming as hard as I could, and was still barely keeping my head an inch above water at times; sometimes even on the best days,

I still went to sleep at night completely drained. But not being able to offer my gratitude left me feeling that things were unfinished. Still, the logistics of completion were a little daunting. I didn't have many of the addresses of those who had helped me. And remembering how long it took me to write the card and book inscription for Chaplain Williams, I didn't know how I could have possibly worked my way through a stack of thank-you notes, even if they came pre-addressed. But still: I was brought up to believe that expressing appreciation is nonnegotiable.

Then, I was suddenly presented with several opportunities to correct this, and taking part in what I've dubbed my "Gratitude Tours" has been one of the most impactful and rewarding things I have ever done.

My first opportunity came during spring break my junior year of college, when I traveled back to southern Afghanistan with the Troops First Foundation as part of their Operation Proper Exit (OPE) program. This trip allows injured service members to go back to Afghanistan and Iraq in order to leave the countries on their own terms, rather than on a medevac. While my friends from school headed to Key West or Cancún, I revisited the unrelenting battleground that had changed my life forever. It was a trip designed to bring some closure, and I was deeply grateful for the opportunity.

Still, I was worried. I didn't want to get injured again. I struggled, wondering, if I were to get injured again, would I be able to recover as well and stay as positive as I had the first time? I didn't want to trigger any latent memories I'd managed to forget. I didn't want to be "different" anymore—hadn't I finally earned the right to be a typical guy, enjoying my twenties?

But the moment I stepped out of the plane, back onto the soil of Afghanistan, everything changed. That country will be a part of me and my story forever. It was exactly the place I needed to be. I made the trip along with four Army Rangers who were also part of OPE. Talk about being outnumbered! I thought I had heard all of the jokes about Marines until I spent a week with them.

They were awesome guys, though. One was a superlative soldier and fellow Medal of Honor recipient, Leroy Petry. One day, we were on a helicopter bound for Kabul. It's difficult to describe the size and grandeur of the Hindu Kush mountain range, which stretches into northern Afghanistan; I felt like we were the size of a Hot Wheels toy helicopter, just a speck in the vastness of it all. As we cruised through the mountains and over the valleys, Petry got an evil grin on his face. He had noticed one of his fellow Rangers, Ralph Joseph, was asleep. Ralph had been shot in the leg on his deployment when an AK-47 round came up through the floor of his helicopter. So, just as if we were on a casual road trip back in the States, Petry realized it was his duty as a friend to mess with Ralph. Petry leaned over to one of the door gunners who was manning a .50-caliber machine gun and whispered his plan. Without hesitation, the door gunner smiled back, pointed his weapon in the air, and unloaded a burst of machine-gun ammo. I thought Ralph was going to jump right out of his seat belt and through the roof of the helo. We all shared a great laugh together—even Ralph. In such a surreal place, with injuries it was hard to believe we'd survived, we were still all just a bunch of guys hanging out and messing with each other. It was nice to feel normal.

We spoke at the embassy and visited the troops there, which was a great experience. But most healing for me was getting to see the ICU bed at the hospital where I was resuscitated the first time, at Camp Bastion. As we walked the halls of the Level 3 military medical facility, I was introduced to one of the radiologists. A few minutes into our conversation, he asked me, "Would you like to see your X-rays from when you came through?"

I thought I had misunderstood him: "Wait, you still have my X-rays from four years ago?!"

He confirmed that they did. Of course I wanted to see them. As I looked at those images, I was once again overcome by the unimaginable work combat doctors, nurses, and medics do every single day—and the fact that I was only standing there because they had somehow managed to do the impossible. I did gain a great deal of closure on that trip, but I also suddenly understood that I had many more loose ends than I realized. My Gratitude Tour had to continue.

Following Operation Proper Exit, I found myself wanting to understand more about those weeks when I was in a coma, and to thank the people who had sustained my life during that time. Three years later, I had the opportunity when the Semper Fi Fund invited me to make the trip back to Landstuhl, in Germany.

More than a decade earlier, the Semper Fi Fund partnered with the Fisher House Foundation, and together, they reached out to the ICU staff at Landstuhl Regional Medical Center to ask what they could do to help the hospital. Since they were anticipating that the request would be some sort of medical equipment to assist with the rapidly growing number of casualties passing through their doors from Iraq and Afghanistan, the response surprised and inspired them. "Bring the soldiers and Marines back," was the immediate answer.

The staff had so many injured people coming through who were only there for a few days or even a few hours that they never got to know the rest of their stories. *Did he make it? Were they able to save the leg? How is she doing now?* The grueling hours and non-stop parade of traumatic injuries can really take a toll on medical professionals; all they got to see was usually just the worst part of the story—the bloodiest, rawest, most horrific scenes. I imagine it would be like watching the opening scenes of hundreds of action movies and never getting to know what happens next or how the story resolves . . . only about a thousand times worse because the people, the blood, and the conflict are real. The staff had watched heartbroken as family members flew over to say goodbye to their loved ones who were not going to make it. Now they wanted to see some of the service members who *did* survive—whose lives they had helped save at Landstuhl.

The Semper Fi Fund and the Fisher House Foundation went to work planning the first trip, which proved to be such an impactful experience that SFF decided it needed to become an annual event. Most of the staff had changed over, as is the nature of military life: People transfer in and out of duty stations. But still, the effect of that first visit on the staff was unforgettable. Amazingly, a nurse happened to still be there from when one of the Marines on my tour had passed through, and even though he had not been conscious at the time, he remembered the sound of her voice and was finally able to pair a face with the words of care and comfort his brain had filed away. It not only encouraged the hospital staff, it provided closure for the service members.

I was invited to be part of the tour in April 2018, and—completely by coincidence—Ryan Craig was on it with me; it was Ryan's mother, Jennifer, who held both of our hands on the flight home from Germany in 2010. Each service member can invite one family member, and Ryan and I both elected to have our mothers come along. It had been a few years since my mom and Jennifer had seen each other, and they cried and hugged like they were old friends who had walked through hell together. In a way, they had.

Each group consisted of about a half-dozen service members and their guests, and together we were taken around the facilities at Landstuhl and talked through exactly how we would have been brought in and what our treatment would have looked like. As we were walking through the ICU, one of the housekeepers—a local German woman who had worked at the base for years—recognized one of the guys in our group and started crying as she walked over to hug him hard, because she had always wondered whether he had made it or not. Her quiet daily tasks of cleaning rooms may have been easy to overlook, but her heart was with the patients as much as anyone else's at Landstuhl, and her dedication to her job and that investment in our lives was a vital part of our care and recovery.

We also had an opportunity to see a dust-off helicopter like the ones that first lift many of our injured troops out of theater to our field hospitals. Exploring them, we could get a fuller picture of the stories most of us had heard only secondhand, from the people who had loaded in our stretchers. In fact, each of us had time to sit quietly in the helicopter by ourselves to just absorb the magnitude of our journey. Although I can recall nothing of my evacuation, for others, it was a significant memory.

"I remember staring at that ceiling and wondering if this would be the last thing I ever saw," one of the guys remarked afterward.

It was a wonderful week—a celebration of life and the people we have become thanks in no small part to the tireless work of the extraordinary network of pilots, crews, medics, nurses, doctors, surgeons, chaplains, administrators, maintenance staff, as well as everyone who makes *their* jobs possible. But what was more, it gave us, the former patients—the ones who are usually recognized and honored for our service—a chance to applaud *our* heroes.

My head was reeling for weeks after that trip; a lot of loose ends in my life were finally getting tied up. There was a feeling of lightness, like a burden had been lifted from me, knowing that I had finally been able to give some small measure back to the community that saved my life. I know I can never fully repay what I owe them. I just hope the staff at Landstuhl understood how deeply appreciative I will always be for everything they did.

Seven months later, in November, the Semper Fi Fund helped me track down the medevac crew who had flown Nick and me from the battlefield, and I was able to meet with them at Nellis Air Force Base in Nevada, which was the home base for their unit. Several members were still in the military, but others who had gotten out since 2010 flew in specifically for our reunion.

If you were injured in Afghanistan, you might get picked up by any one of three different types of teams; the Army has what they call their "dust-off" crews, the Air Force has "Pedro," and occasionally the British might step in with their teams, nicknamed "Tricky." Whoever got you, though, the mission was the same: to quickly and safely evacuate casualties while protecting the crews loading and treating the people on board. Nick and I were evacuated by two sets of incredible Air Force Pedro teams. Pararescue jumpers (PJs) will exit from the bird after landing with their weapons and help the troops on the ground set up security while the patients are loaded; meanwhile, door gunners on 50-caliber machine guns stay on board to keep their weapons pointed down once the chopper takes back off to help prevent any ground-to-air interference. I'd always been curious about these men and women who risked their lives to get me to safety, and now, at last, I was getting the chance to meet them . . . But what do you say in a situation like that? "Thank you" just doesn't seem sufficient.

I was picked up at the Las Vegas airport by Jasper Heilig, a former Marine who now works with the Semper Fi Fund and is a vital part of pulling together reunions like these and events like the Landstuhl trip. He drove me over to the base, where the crew was waiting in a conference room. We went around the table and everyone introduced themselves: Jewell Steamer, Wes Loignon, Kevin Holland, Paul Sheehey, Brian Rhoades, Zachary Ferguson, Kyle Waite, Joshua Ramsey, and Corey Kuttie. They all told me how happy they were to be there, but I was a bit overwhelmed. Finally, I just looked at them and said, "What can you possibly say to someone who saved your life? No words will ever come close to expressing what you deserve." I tried to tell them how much they meant, not only to my family and me, but also to the thousands of other people whose stories they are now a part of thanks to their exhaustive work, remarkable bravery, and willingness to sacrifice themselves emotionally by inserting themselves into battle day in and day out.

The crew was great; a few admitted that they didn't remember me specifically (and why should they, given the hundreds of medevacs they had completed each month during that time?), but a number of them did, because a hand-grenade blast stood out among the IED and bullet wounds they were more used to seeing. One of the PJs told me the injuries to my face were so extensive that he would never forget how I looked. I was classified as a C-Cat, which is the most severe level of casualty, and any activity in the air at that time is dedicated to covering and evacuating the casualty. In fact, I was only the second C-Cat my Pedro crew had ever heard from who survived.

I learned stories about the day of my injury—eight years later—that I'd never heard before. For example, even though I remember feeling myself slip away before my buddies loaded me onto the chopper, I was awake and apparently pretty feisty during the flight. Every time they tried to insert a CRIC to help my breathing, just as Doc Frend had contemplated, I apparently fought them off and kept trying to lie on my side, facing the door where the gunners were—and Jewell was one of the gunners. The crew laughingly told me I was probably just doing that so I could look at Jewell because I hadn't seen a woman in four months. I have absolutely no recollection of anything during the flight, so I was fascinated to hear that not only were my eyes open, but I was physically pushing the crew away like a little kid fighting his mom who is trying to spoon peas into his mouth. Finally, they gave up on the CRIC because I seemed to be handling my breathing situation okay on my own—at least, I was getting enough oxygen to keep flipping over to my side.

Incredibly, it took only thirty-six minutes from the moment they got the call to the moment they handed me off at the field hospital, where the doctors praised them for doing so little to me—which sounds like a horrible thing to say but was actually a huge compliment. Doc Frend had done such an amazing job patching me up on the ground before I was loaded onto the bird and the Pedro crew had done exactly the right thing in not forcing a CRIC when I fought them. This made the job of the field docs much easier; there was no additional trauma caused by triage measures to staunch bleeding or create emergency airways. Against all odds, my first responders managed to keep me alive.

The very helicopter that transported me out of Marjah is still in use today (it was built in 1978, so it's seen a lot of action!) and I was able to step into and out of it on my own two feet that morning in Nevada. The bird that had picked up Nick immediately afterward was still in service, too, until just recently, when it crashed on the range during a training exercise. Someone salvaged a piece of the body and had a plaque mounted on it that reads:

On 21 November 2010 two United States Air Force rescue helicopters, call sign "Pedro," launched on MM(SW)11-21D from Camp Bastion to save two critically wounded United States Marines from Patrol Base Dakota, Marjah District, Helmand Province, Afghanistan. The swift and efficient actions of the crews ultimately resulted in saving the lives of the two Marines.

It was inscribed with my name and Nick's, and the Pedro logo and motto: "The things we do . . . that others may live." They presented it in honor of both Nick and me. It was incredible to think of all the lives that were saved as a result of that machine and those people standing with me. The pilots and the gunners, the medics and maintenance crews, the guy whose job it was to rinse the blood out of the bird after each mission—they were no longer faceless parts of my story.

Ironically, given how hard I apparently fought anyone trying to create an artificial airway for me, I feel like I can breathe more easily now having taken these Gratitude Tours. Even if I wasn't always able to meet the exact same people who had worked on me in each location, I was still able to let those present see how much their work matters—not just in a broad, philosophical sense, but to me personally. I owe them a debt I will never be able to repay, but the magnitude of that debt no longer seems as overwhelming now that I have been able to look them in the eye and acknowledge them. It's as if I've no longer just *received* care, but have been able to offer at least something in return.

There is power in moving from someone who only receives to someone who is able to give, too. For me, it marked a major shift in my view of myself and my view of the world. Even though my healing journey will never really be over, the opportunities I've had to thank people have helped me move beyond the chapter of my life dedicated to recovery; now, I can look ahead to whatever comes next, making something out of this life that so many people worked to save.

The healing power of saying thank you is immense; I believe this with every ounce of my being. Whether to a teacher or a parent or a mentor or a friend or a pastor or a health-care provider or a quiet supporter or an entire community, there is freedom that comes with expressing appreciation. It is acknowledging their role in the progress you've made from "there" to "here," whatever that may look like for you. It closes the loop.

I can't imagine anything more beautiful in this world than gratitude—feeling it, expressing it, receiving it. Gratitude is at the heart of every "Thank you for your service" that someone offers to a veteran. I understand the feeling of not knowing what to say, but wanting to say *something,* because the gift that was given is too significant to go unacknowledged. I appreciate the gratitude that is shared with me, but I hope people know that I *owe* so much more thanks than I will ever be able to express.

Gratitude, I've come to learn, is one of the most important parts of becoming a whole person and building a life of significance. Gratitude requires wisdom to recognize the roles of others; it requires humility to admit you couldn't have done it alone; it requires strength to be able to give part of yourself back to someone and know there is still enough of you left to thrive; and it requires inner peace to be able to say, "What you did for me helped create a life I am glad to call mine."

Parting Thoughts

I am asked all the time, "How did you do what you did?" The question is almost always followed by the declaration: "I don't think I could have covered a grenade for someone."

I have two responses to that.

The first is that I don't recommend falling on a grenade, period.

The second is a little more complex, and it has to do with the beauty of the human spirit: I don't know if I could have done it, either, if I had had time to stop and really think about it. As I shared at the beginning of the book, when Nick and I were on the roof the day before, discussing what we would do if a grenade landed up there with us, he said, "My ass is off this f——ing roof," and I told him, "I'm right behind you!"

In other words, the idea of doing something heroic never crossed my mind.

Then what happened, happened.

Before I found myself in the situation, I don't think I could have said with any confidence that I would have ever considered covering a grenade. But, as the saying goes, "Desperate times call for desperate measures." Our brain can evaluate situations and prompt our body to react before our conscious mind fully grasps what is happening. We react instinctively, and I am just grateful that I grew up surrounded by others who helped shape those instincts to be steered by loyalty and commitment to the things and people that matter.

I don't remember much about the incident and I definitely don't remember what I was thinking in the moment, but, again, that's the amazing thing about people: You never know how you're going to step up, or when.

I'm proud of what I did, but at the same time, I'm surprised by it. My guess is that you have surprised yourself, too—that there have been times when you didn't put much forethought into the moment but, looking back, you realize just how boldly you acted. It may have been the action of a moment or it could have been the strength and persistence of weathering a particularly difficult season in your life. As you reflect on it now, you are probably surprised at what you were capable of enduring. The fallout of that time for you might not be as readily obvious as mine was, but the idea is the same: You did what you had to do and you made your world—our world—a little bit better. That's courage. That's heroism. That's honor.

Thank you for your service.

Acknowledgments

My life began when I was born, but my opportunity for a second chance and self-discovery began after I woke up from the devastating blast of an enemy hand grenade. The words in between the covers of this book have been meticulously crafted to tell you of a journey. This is not about a moment; it is about a journey that is greater than any single person or experience. It is a journey that evolved through years of struggle, self-reflection, support, and love. It shows that big battles are accomplished by accumulating small victories and even the smallest of steps can lead to completion of the grandest journey.

It is a journey of the human spirit.

There wasn't a definitive moment in which I knew that I was going to write this book. But if there had been, it likely would have been the moment a couple of years ago when a fellow Marine approached me in a receiving line and told me that though he had been struggling with depression after coming back from war, he didn't kill himself because he had been following my story and it had been his inspiration. Wow, suddenly sharing this meant more than I realized. I know that although every struggle is individually specific, struggle (mentally, physically, or emotionally) is a universally understood language. Since that moment with that Marine, I have relentlessly thought about how I could put my experiences and the lessons I have learned from those experiences into words that everyone can understand, relate to, and, most important, learn from.

The lessons of life, silver linings, and perspective that I share in this book did not come easily or quickly. At times, silver linings only became apparent because I was forced to search through darkness. And perspectives only became clear after years of deep thought and personal growth. These lessons originated from pain and suffering. But sometimes the most difficult struggles teach us the most beautiful lessons.

Most important, I must acknowledge that this book

and even my second chance at life would not be possible without the countless people who have unquestionably given their time, energy, and effort to help me get to where I am today. From the medevac crews who risked their lives to save mine, to the medical staff that continued to resuscitate me when there was no life left, to the Walter Reed National Military Medical Center family who spent three years helping heal and reconstruct my torn apart body, to the Semper Fi fund and other nonprofits that selflessly gave my parents money and resources so my parents could comfortably stay by my bedside while I continued to fight, to the Fisher House Foundation who always opened its welcoming doors of love to my family, to the Marines who have loved and supported me from my first day at boot camp, to my drill instructors who worked exhaustively to give me the foundation and mold me into the best United States Marine I could become, to my tutor that traveled to the hospital every day to help me prepare for my transition into college, to my college professors that helped me earn my degree that I am so very proud of, to the wonderful people in my home state of South Carolina who have been there since my first day out of the hospital, to the Sentinels of Freedom foundation and its investors who assisted me financially through college, to the mentors who continue to help me grow professionally, to the Lexington (S.C.) Medical Center employees who treated me like more than a patient, to the Augusta, Georgia, burn center employees who patiently spent hours cleaning my wounds for the seven months I was away from Walter Reed and at home recovering, to my childhood teachers and coaches, to so many members of my extended family such as aunts and cousins who drove from Mississippi to take shifts taking care of me in the hospital so mom and dad could rest and shifts staying with my brothers at our home in South Carolina while they continued high school, to my grandmothers who helped change my diapers, and to my friends who have loved me and helped pick me up when I have stumbled, I sincerely thank you from the bottom of my heart.

Lastly, there is the team that brought this book to life. To Don Yaeger and Tiffany Brooks, thank you. Thank you for intently listening to me throughout our fifteen months of writing. Thank you for all the encouragement you constantly gave me. Thank you for welcoming my 2:00 a.m. "idea" emails. Thank you for always working hard to make sure that I was comfortable with every word that went on paper and that my book was written with the utmost respect. Most importantly, thank you for being my friends.

To our agent, Ian Kleinert, and to Peter Hubbard, Nick Amphlett, and the HarperCollins and William Morrow publishing family, I sincerely thank you for believing in my journey. From the moment this book, and our journey together, began you have shown me nothing but enthusiasm, love, and support. I am truly appreciative.

To Don, Tiffany, Ian, Peter, HarperCollins, and William Morrow, from the moment I started making notes for a potential book my goal has been to help people and, to whatever extent I can, impact the world. Because of your belief in me and all your hard work, I believe we are going to do just that.

This story is not just mine. It is a journey and a triumph for everyone and I am truly honored and humbled to have you a part of it forever.

—Kyle